GETTING UNSTUCK WITHOUT COMING UNGLUED

Francy Starr

Merlin Design – 2012

DEDICATION

To my Sweet Sixteen

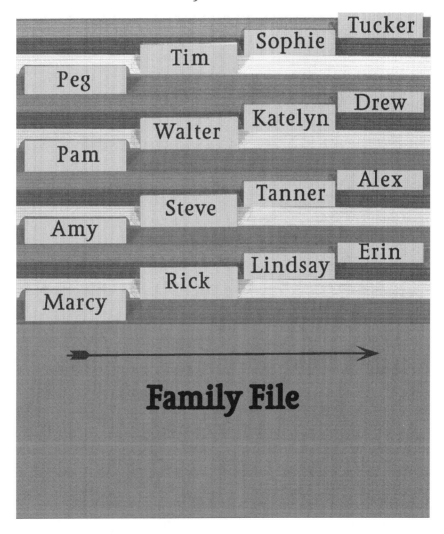

TABLE OF CONTENTS

CHAPTER I

BOOKENDS

Sex and riding a bicycle are two things you're never supposed to forget. It's not true. I damn near forgot how to ride a bicycle!

Having just moved to California in the early eighties, I joined a singles biking group. It seemed a good way to meet people, while moving forward with my life.

To look trendy, I updated my old riding garb with a new sweat band. Speeding along, I tugged at it nervously. It felt wringing wet - and I was still in my car! I hadn't been on a bike in years and was terrified.

At the rental shop, I mounted the new model gingerly. With my bottom perched high on the seat mid-air, and my arms stretched taut to reach the handlebars, I felt like I was in traction - already. Maybe it was the strange push-pull effect. I pushed the pedals; the bike pulled my neck, my muscles and my back. I had as much confidence of my safe return as a kamikaze pilot. Oh well. Sometimes walking is a risk.

At first, the bike lurched in all directions. Then suddenly it took off and began zooming full speed along San Diego's crowded boardwalk on Mission Beach.

A man, astonished, raced to catch up. "Hey, a few minutes ago you were afraid to get on that thing. Now you're out here ahead of everybody."

Without turning, I shot back, "I have to go fast; otherwise, I'll fall off."

Immediately it struck me - that's what I was doing with my life!

The trial separation from my husband had been a trial, all right. Desperate, I was trying therapy, seminars, workshops and courses to decipher the past and explore my future. And for the present, I was joining every singles group in town. On a frantic marathon, I felt exhausted. Whizzing through life ten-speed is absurd, I decided - but a fraction too late. Three skaters and I collided and all fell together in a tangled heap.

"Are you okay?" they asked.

"Sure," I answered, yet knew I wasn't. I hurt all over, but not from the fall. With my marriage of thirty-plus years becoming a minus, I'd recently moved from the Midwest to La Jolla, a beautiful beach community adjacent to San Diego. Why not open a new window with an ocean view? I tried to be flippant, but California is a long way from Illinois (especially on a Sunday) and I missed my family and friends.

With nothing broken, except my spirit, I pulled over to a grassy area to brood. I thought about going back to my new one-bedroom condo to call my old four-bedroom house, but told myself no.

With my telephone addiction, main-lining a phone fix would be inevitable. I wanted so much to reach out and touch someone - anyone, but especially my husband, Buddy. I missed him most.

"Unplug," I told myself in the exact tone Lee, my therapist used. Gazing over at the bay, I stretched out on the grass in the warm sunshine and remembered my first session with him.

Wearing tear-stained funereal black silk, I'd trudged into his office, bereaved and maudlin. Scanning the room, I observed the thick textbooks that filled the paneled shelves, and noted the clock on his desk angled out to be seen. I gazed for a long moment at the couch. On the table in front of it, within easy reach, sat a giant-size box of Kleenex, the tissue popped-up and ready. I approved of his layout and gave him "A" for accoutrements. But could he help me?

He greeted me and smiled. I murmured "Hello," and headed for the Kleenex. I sank down on the couch and blew my nose - then, unsure how to begin, blurted out inanely, "I want to have bookends made, with two numbers on each side, 15 and 51." He looked curious so I continued, "I think bronze would be appropriate. Isn't that what they use for caskets?"

He nodded, then asked, "Why?"

"Because the relationship with my husband, Buddy, seems forever. I was fifteen when it began and I'm fifty-one now. It should be in bookends." The dull ache at the back of my neck suddenly sharp, I stopped before adding, "It's my whole life!"

He said in a low, firm voice, "No, it's not your whole life. It was a part of it." He paused. Then deliberately matter-of-fact, he finished, "And now you have the rest of your life to live."

I looked up at him, amazed at how simple it had all become. Feeling reprieved, I thought, the man is brilliant!

"You're right," I exclaimed, and ecstatic, jumped up off the couch and ran out.

And that is *precisely* the way it happened.

However, there is an element of timing to be considered. When I jumped up and ran out – it was a year later. He wanted to hear about my life: my husband, my children and me. I needed his help, so I told him my story.

3

*****

Buddy and I were childhood sweethearts.

On our first date, as we said good night, he whispered nervously, "I don't want to go steady."

"Who wants to go steady?" I replied, fifteen years old.

We made an attractive couple. A handsome high school senior, he had nice eyes and a wonderful smile. I had dark hair and dimples, not matching but cute. My sophomore peers thought I was lucky to be asked out by an "older man." I thought so too, especially one who had a maroon convertible. We began going steady, and soon fell in love.

The next year he went to the University of Illinois, pledged a fraternity and barely received his hard-earned pin before he asked me to wear it.

His whole fraternity serenaded me, with Allan Sherman (who later wrote "Hello Muddah, Hello Faddah") singing a new parody he'd written for my pinning. "Don't Fence Me In" became "Don't Take My Pin." God, it was fun!

By the time I got to the U. of I. two years later, Buddy was due to leave for the service.

"I should use the time you're away to go out with others so I'll know if I really love you," I told him, combining logic with high school theatrics. I had never dated anyone else (unless you count social dancing in junior high school).

He agreed reluctantly and had his fraternity pin made into a ring with a gold cap fit to cover it. We would still be pinned, but in secret. How clandestine, I thought, and pictured myself wearing the ring dressed in a London Fog trench coat with the collar turned up.

From overseas, Buddy wrote "Dear Mom" letters to my mother, who in turn wrote him tips on how to land me.

"Don't send her a birthday present," she advised, "not even a telegram." They always had a great relationship - and love each other even now.

At school, I dated several boys rather seriously whose last names began with "M" as did Buddy's. I wrote home jokingly that we could start monogramming linens and lingerie. I knew what my last initial would be. I could figure out the name later.

Buddy came back from Guam a lean 165 pounds, his hair streaked blonde from the sun. He walked into my house a hero; smiled broadly, hugged me closely and kissed me passionately. After he put down his pipe.

He asked me to marry him. How could I say no? But when I requested more time, he said, "Fine," and asked out my best friend. God, my mother was smart!

Buddy and I married on my twentieth birthday, settled in our home town and started our life together. Everyone was delighted. We were happy, too. I was a monogram at last.

Being married felt wonderful. We found making love legally

to be extra special. When we came up for air, Buddy began a business and I finished school. We played bridge and golf together, and took a Great Books course at the library. We soon began to feel like old marrieds, but still held hands at the movies.

At my college graduation the next year, the cap and gown felt doubly heavy over my maternity dress. As the valedictorian delivered her address, "Starting Life," I felt the first kick. The other speeches went on ad nauseam - or maybe it was my morning sickness. I felt dizzy marching out up the long aisle, and when Buddy snapped my picture, I thought, "So much for Pomp and Circumstance."

Within eight years we had four daughters. At the birth of our last, our babysitter phoned to ask if we realized we'd had our fourth child, fourth daughter, on the fourth day of the fourth month. We hadn't even thought of it.

Buddy laughed and said, "Gee, we planned that well, didn't we?" Together we marveled that the rhythm system - a bit out of sync - could produce such uncanny timing. Actually we felt lucky and grateful to have our special surprise baby and healthy children. With our family complete, we loved each other even more.

Of course, our lives became focused on the girls. The Great Books were shelved higher to make room for bottles and diapers, toys and games, and an endless succession of dolls.

From early on, our refrigerator door was the established place for "show and tell," and it became custom for all family kudos to be duly posted. We thought it supportive, and more appropriate than sending out braggadocio stories with Christmas cards.

It had been easy with just one child. "Marcy loves to color," a purple bunny report from her pre-school, went up first, all alone on the bare white door.

"Amy draws well," was next.

Later on, as our daughters grew in number and accomplishment, we couldn't get a glass of milk without the fridge door falling off (or so it seemed). We put up everything.

At the top went the articles Pam and Peg wrote for their underground - but aboveboard – junior high school newspaper. Their views on freedom, justice and abortion showed sensitivity and integrity, even at an early age. Buddy and I were happy our kids were developing into nice people.

There were hectic moments in our family, but after the smoke cleared from our battles, there remained much love among us. Besides loving our kids, we liked them, too. They were great fun to live with and helped make our lives interesting and meaningful.

All too soon the time came when, one by one, they were ready to go off to college. As we hugged each daughter farewell, Buddy gave last minute counseling in finance, economics, and checks and balances.

I gave them a mother's potpourri of caution, advice, possible remedies for improbable diseases and other general words of wisdom. My basic message was always the same, "There's a whole world out there - go find it."

When our last daughter left, and our oldest got married, the empty nest syndrome came home to roost. But what was so terrible? We had more closets, more bathrooms - more space. It was

great, and we were fine. We clucked contentedly and settled in.

There were wonderful new-found freedoms. We could walk around the house in the nude, and decide dinner - food, time and place - at the last minute. (Do you say order in, or order out?) But the real fun was being able to choose what we wanted to do now that PTA meetings, swim meets and other child-oriented activities were over.

To me there was a sweetness about it. I felt it to be one of the most beautiful segments of life. The denouement, the sunset. Everything in pinks, purples and lavenders. How rosy it was. For a while.

Maybe it was too much of a good thing. It reminded me of the story of a small child in a free school who asked his teacher, "Do we *have* to do just exactly what we want, again *today?*" Perhaps in that question, really a statement of despair, lays the germination of the now rampant disease, mid-life crisis.

I have an overview of the malaise. In retrospect.

People at mid-life aren't always sure how to enjoy their newly free world sans children, at least for very long. Usually they begin, innocently enough, to question life in depth: "What's it all about, Alfie?" kind of stuff.

Sometimes that can be healthy, but when mixed with desperate thoughts such as "We're not getting any younger," it's usually not.

Often depression sets in, which leads to another question: "Is this all there is?" If asked with a nervous cough, that can be ominous.

"Might sex be better with someone else?" induces high fever and is *highly* contagious.

When followed quickly by "You only live once," my advice is take two aspirin and stay *out* of bed. Otherwise, to paraphrase Adelaide in "Guys and Dolls," a marriage . . . could develop a cold.

Atchoo!!

One day we woke up with sniffles - and our marriage wasn't feeling well either. With red eyes and runny noses we took it to a marriage counselor who confirmed our fears. Sounding grim he told us, "You have a severe case of classic mid-life crisis."

I groaned. Did we have to be so classic?

I turned to Buddy and tried to be funny through tears. "Well, you said from the beginning you didn't want to go steady." He gave me an uncomfortable half-smile, then looked away.

I couldn't believe what was happening. I stared at him and thought, "Oh Buddy, how can you love someone else? You've always loved me!"

I remembered how, long ago, he had pursued me, and tried so hard to convince me that I loved him. I wanted to shout, "Hey Buddy! You convinced me! I'm convinced! Here I am and I love you more than ever!" But the words stayed stuck and my throat felt sore.

Our relationship had not only shifted, but had begun to tilt precariously. Space seemed necessary so we opted for a trial separation. It had been a long marriage, and we felt we owed each other that. Perhaps time and distance would be good for us. Oh God, I prayed, please let him miss me.

As we'd planned, Buddy packed and left while I was away from the house. When I returned, the emptiness hit me the moment I opened the door. He had left home before on business or errands, but this time it was different. He was gone.

I found living alone miserable. The big house and the small town didn't fit together, or measure up to the dimension I wanted for my life.

Buddy's office in our home presented an added problem. On week days he needed to be there. Sometimes we'd converge in the den.

"How are you?" he'd ask.

"OK," I'd lie, "how about you?"

"Not well," he'd admit.

We'd hug and kiss and cry - and move in different directions.

Because our home housed his office, and since the girls were grown and gone, it seemed logical to me that I should be the one to leave. Buddy could come back, have his office available and water my plants. He agreed the plan made sense, and it became a mutual decision.

As the news of our separation spread, I began receiving "condolence" calls from incredulous friends. Many marriages were dissolving, but how could ours? We'd always been so much in love. Was nothing sacred anymore?

My friend, Bev, suggested that, like a Bible story, it was a plague that would pass over.

I said, "Let us pray." We bowed our heads in mock reverence, then tried to laugh, but couldn't.

Horrified and grief-stricken, the girls came home to offer their love and support to us both. It was awful for them. There was nothing they could do. One day, in desperation, all four together tried cooking chicken soup. Hearing their voices in the kitchen brought back a flood of memories, and convinced me more than ever that leaving the house was right for me.

I made the decision to take a trip alone at first. I needed space and time away from the house and phone, my children and friends, to sort things out for myself. Then I planned to circle around, visiting family.

I remembered a quote from Goethe once posted on our refrigerator: "Whatever you can do or dream you can, begin it. Boldness has genius, power and magic in it."

I didn't feel overwhelmed with power, but just making a decision, knew I'd begun - and I felt better.

I still had no idea where I'd land. I'd figure that out later. "It's an adventure," I told myself. Thinking of the early explorers, I had misgivings. How the hell had they done it? Yet, if they made it without falling off the Earth, so could I.

Before leaving I went to the doctor and the dentist. I got new glasses and a new umbrella. I felt much the same as I did before leaving my parents, hurrying to have them take final care of me.

I also grocery shopped to fill the fridge and freezer. God forbid Buddy should go hungry!

On impulse, I fixed a meatloaf, his favorite dish. He used to complain I didn't make it often enough. It was the best farewell present I could think of.

I walked around the house one last time, stopping for a moment in the den. I loved the way the sun came through the windows. It was everyone's favorite room. Even though it was small with only two chairs and an ottoman, Buddy would say to the kids, "Pull up the floor and sit down." It never failed to get a laugh, and we'd all squeeze in.

I looked at the family pictures interspersed among the books, and the clock that Buddy and I had bought in Switzerland. We used to close the den doors at night so we wouldn't hear it chime. I knew I'd miss it.

I went upstairs quickly to collect my things. The girls all hovered around to help, trying to be brave.

"Be sure to let us know where you are, Mom," said Marcy.

"Try to establish credit right away," Amy advised.

Pam, who had the most traffic tickets, cautioned, "Remember, Mom, you speed up to get on a freeway, not slow down."

Peggy, my youngest, put her arms around me and said, "You'll make it, Mom."

We all cried together as they walked me to the door, but somehow the role reversal made us laugh too. I suddenly had four mothers hugging me farewell, giving me advice and encouragement.

"Be careful, but go for it," they were saying. Translated, the message was still the same, "There's a whole world out there, go find it!"

CHAPTER II

WHERE'S SAN DIEGO?

Traveling solo for the first time, I wound up in a small resort hotel in Wisconsin. The trip crossed over more than a state border. It became a journey into my new, single world.

Luggage, reservations and tipping had always been handled by Buddy. Not until I struggled to locate lost luggage, rearrange wrong reservations and tip from the top of my head, did I fully appreciate all he had done with ease.

As I waited in the hotel lobby for my room (not available for two hours) I began to experience a frustrating mixture of emotions. I tried to be grateful for Buddy's taking charge through the years, but felt resentful more. So inept at managing everything alone now, I felt hassled, and short-changed by my lack of experience. I was upset with Buddy for spoiling me, and angry with myself for allowing it.

Embarrassed by my unworldliness, I vowed to get savvy, and become a competent, veteran traveler. Never again would I set out in a car with a low tire, dressed in a white linen suit, carrying nothing smaller than $20 bills.

Dining alone was the worst experience of all. You can put your hands on a roll and butter knife, but where do you put your eyes? I found a place. But how long can you look at lettuce?

When you look up, what then? I didn't know whether to gaze

around the room or glance at people. Is it rude to read? What should your countenance be? A smile could seem suggestive, a frown, unfriendly. I strived for noncommittal nonchalance, but never made it.

When I was brought the menu, I studied it intently, grateful for a place to focus. After ordering, and it was pulled from my hands, I eyed the dessert cart at the next table. When that was carted off, I examined the china. Then I watched the ice melt in my glass. Ill at ease with my wedding ring off, I felt an odd creature - married, yet single, in a new society I didn't like.

A man glanced at me and grinned.

I looked at my lettuce a long time, gulped dinner when it arrived and went to my room.

Slamming my door and locking it, I remembered our family's basic message: There's a whole world out there - go find it! Lonesome in my empty room, I realized the world I was finding was dismal.

I thought of all the times I had wanted to be alone, away from crying babies and responsibilities. I even remembered those dark, secret moments when I'd fantasized being with a man other than Buddy, safe from discovery in a far-off hotel room.

Well, I was alone and responsible only for myself. In my secluded hotel room, I could do anything I wanted. But, the thought of sex with another man was repugnant and I fantasized being at home with my husband.

I cried hard and slept fitfully on "Buddy's side" of the bed.

The next morning after breakfast (in my room) I went for a walk around the grounds. This was the space and time I had wanted for myself and oh, how I needed it!

I came to the middle of a woodsy area overlooking a lake and sat down. After checking carefully to make sure no one was nearby, I began to talk out loud to myself. I spoke as I would to a friend in trouble, "You *have* been through a lot, poor dear. It's been horrid, hasn't it?" I even allowed bitter tears for a long while. I hoped to get out my sadness if I could, but the tears seemed non-stop. Then I became chastising, "Come on, Francy, get with it. You've had more than enough 'poor me' time; let's move on." I knew I was right.

Finally, after getting control of myself, I tried putting my "heads" together to figure out what to do with my life. The sound of my voice gave me added strength, and somehow I seemed to be getting through to myself. I hoped I wasn't schizo. But I needed to become a functioning person again - even at the risk of becoming dichotomous - I told myself.

I knew I must think seriously about finding a place to live. I remembered the game Buddy and I had invented for long car trips. We'd take turns conjuring up exotic places we could retire to someday, and loved to speculate where we'd find our most glorious spot. I tried thinking of some place for me now, but playing alone, the game was no fun.

Still, I closed my eyes and conjured up Tahiti, Barbados and the south of France, but ruled them out fast. Who was I kidding? They were wonderful places to vacation, but unrealistic for me now. Besides, who knew what my financial position would be? Searching for my most glorious spot, I'd need to be practical.

I got up, found a winding path in the woods and followed it. My plan to circle around, visiting family, remained the most sensible. Looking down at the lake, I realized I'd always wanted to live near water. I was lucky to have relatives in L.A., Miami and Sarasota.

I'd been glad, too, when a friend had suggested I visit her daughter, Annie, in San Diego. I said, "Sure...where's San Diego?" and added it to my list. I vaguely remembered water around there somewhere.

Wondering how I'd pick the place best for me, I grew jittery. I thought of our old Airedale, Oliver, who used to wind around in a circle until he found the perfect place comfortable to plop. Would it be like that for me? My gut feeling told me I'd need more than instinct.

I went back to my room to devise a plan. I decided to research each city visited by investigating places to live, work and worship. I'd explore lifestyles and single scenes, too. Surely it made sense to learn about a community before choosing it for a home.

To get set for the task, I went to a drugstore and equipped

myself with legal pads, pencils and *lots* of erasers. I felt on track - but not infallible. Next, I checked schedules, my family's and the airlines', then planned my itinerary.

Formulating a strategy created a purpose for my traveling. As I began making notes on the first page of the top legal pad, I felt in charge and sensed a new direction in my life.

The tears that night weren't desperate, just sad. I slept better, and on my side of the bed. The next morning I got up early to drive home, repack and begin my adventure.

*****

It started in L.A. with my eldest daughter and her husband, Rick, my son-in-law, the psychologist. Marcy, pregnant with my first grandchild, mothered me well, and we talked more woman talk than ever before. She was understanding and sympathetic, yet had a realistic approach to problem-solving that was good for me. Steady as you go, that's Marcy.

Although reticent to enter into family affairs, Rick offered off-the-cuff general therapy and advice. Once I told him about a dream I'd had. In it I bodily picked up the "other woman" and threw her out of a window. I woke up furious because it was only a one-story building.

"Why couldn't it have been a skyscraper?" I asked him.

"Because you really don't want to kill her."

"The hell I don't!" I retorted. We both laughed, he more than I.

I stayed with Amy in L.A. too. We had long one-to-one gab sessions that were great. Late nights were spent talking about the clashes we'd had between us.

She reminded me of the time I took her to a counselor who gave her finger paints to draw Mommy. When she drew me as a witch, I demanded, "Where are *my* finger paints?" (There were a few years we didn't get along well.)

Now with new awareness and understanding, we worked through past hurts, developing a present bond, close and special. We finally got to know each other for the first time in twenty years.

One night we hugged hard, feeling love and genuine affection for each other. Then, misty-eyed, I said, "Amy, let's make hot cocoa with marshmallows like we used to when you were little."

She stood up laughing and said, "Hell, Mom, Let's go bar hopping!" (I realized that since my separation, I'd transcended far beyond being a mere mother figure.)

I laughed too, and said, "Why not?"

She pulled on her boots. I pulled up my girdle. Then, arm in arm, mother and daughter went out on the town.

Cruising the L.A. scene with Amy, I took special note of pink hair and punk rock, good jazz and bad booze - white wine and rhinestone cowboys. I thought people moved fast on the freeways, but they moved even faster in the bars.

The next morning when I checked my computer print-out sheet (a page from my legal pad), L.A. showed up too much for me. I decided I needed a quiet visit with my mother in Florida.

Miami Beach was lovelier on the bay side away from the tourist strip, I noticed, but it still didn't feel right for me. Discouraged and tired from L.A., I slumped into a state of depression.

Mom comforted me the way she used to when I was a little girl, hugging me and stroking my forehead. Later, we talked about when Dad died, and how awful and alone she'd felt. No longer the little girl, I understood more than ever.

While there, I called a college chum in Miami, and told her I was surveying her city and why. We met for dinner at a local "meat market," probably so dubbed for all the flank steak on the hoof around the bar.

We had drinks at a ringside table to observe the single scene in action. We saw young men with young women, middle-age men with young women - and old men with young women.

I said, "God, it's depressing, isn't it?"

She said, "Yes, but I wanted you to get the picture."

The picture was so graphic there was no need for notes.

We caught up on each other's lives; she told me her first husband had died early, leaving her with three small children. She had divorced her second husband several years ago. Just recently he'd committed suicide.

My being in the throes of a divorce after a reasonably happy marriage of thirty-one years suddenly seemed not so horrible, and barely worth discussing.

We ordered a good bottle of wine with dinner, and both got a little drunk. It felt wonderful, even worth the hangover the next day.

From Miami, I flew to Sarasota to visit my brother and sister-in-law, and explore their town. They met me with open arms which I fell into gratefully.

I had private quarters, even a lush patio outside my room where I could read, think and talk to myself. It was the first time since Wisconsin I'd had such space and, feeling low, I needed to rev myself up again.

Later I scouted around the city to collect information. The gulf was gorgeous, and I began to perk up. But discovering devastating data (their middle-age singles ranged from sixty-five to *God*), I became aghast, then wilted immediately. My Cross pen, upset, recorded the sad note. Even the paper crumpled in sympathy.

Running out of out-of-state relatives, I decided to visit my friend's daughter, Annie, and San Diego. I flew back to L.A. to go from there.

With my kids my teachers, I practiced driving the freeways, my knuckles white over the wheel. As I drove around scared, I thought of my mother the night of my dad's funeral.

She and Dad had had such a long and special relationship; everyone wondered how she'd make it alone. What would become of this wonderful woman, who could cook and bake magnificently, yet needed to be driven to the grocery store?

As the family all hovered around to tuck her into bed that night, my sister, Estelle, said gently, "You know, Mom, things are going to be different now with Dad gone."

Mom sat up in bed, her big, blue eyes opened wide, and said, "I know, I know – I know," louder each time. She paused slightly, then blurted out, "I just have to ... learn to *drive!*"

And she did, getting her first driver's license at 72.

Two months later, she ran into a boat (in someone's garage) - but by God, she drove.

Now, learning to drive freeways in heavy traffic, I felt inspired by her courage and knew I'd make it, too. But when I noticed a car pulling a boat in the lane ahead, I clutched the wheel tighter, steered to the right and took the first off-ramp I could find, just to make sure.

When finally comfortable with California driving, I made arrangements to rent a car for my trip to San Diego. I felt brave going alone with no family there, and I didn't know Annie very well. But I remembered what I'd told myself in Illinois: It's an adventure.

"I'm ready," I told Marcy, and she drove me to pick up my rental car. When I got behind the wheel, she bent over her pregnant tummy and leaned through my window to "tuck me in." Then she whispered, "Mom, you're not learning how to drive today - you're learning how to fly." We kissed goodbye, and I drove off quickly.

When I got to La Jolla and saw the ocean, I said out loud, "Oh, my God, it's on water!" I walked the first beach I could find and talked to myself. I sounded excited.

I drove around the spectacular scenic routes. My ears popped as I followed a winding road up the mountain, right in the middle of town. Looking down over the curves, I thought I was in Switzerland or Austria and exhilarated, got a ridiculous urge to yodel loudly.

At the top, I parked my car and looked around. To my right, I could see the San Diego skyline, and Mexico in the distance. On the left were the La Jolla shores and the PACIFIC OCEAN! It looked even bigger from higher up. And the sea air smelled crisper than cornfields. I inhaled deeply.

For the first time, I felt real hope thinking, "This might be it!" I stayed in San Diego with Annie and her big sheep dog, Bert, to investigate thoroughly and find out.

Early the next morning, with renewed zeal (and a fresh legal pad) I drove into the village of La Jolla to sniff the air. I stood on a corner and watched the people, smiling and friendly, as they ambled in and out of the low, Spanish-style library. A post office to match was two corners down. I heard there was a town council, and liked the folksy sound of it.

Enjoying the sunshine and the ocean view, I moseyed down to the Cove, then walked up to hotels, restaurants and shops, all overlooking the water. I loved it!

I poked in and out of the boutiques eyeing scanty bathing suits and sexy lace nightgowns. My fantasies traveled ahead to my new single life; then my pulse began racing - to catch up.

At lunch, I savored my mushrooms stuffed with crabmeat. They tasted much more exotic than "Steak 'N Shake" hamburgers. The view of that incredible ocean from my table was glorious. I never once watched the ice in my glass.

In the afternoon I browsed through art galleries. At a bookstore I treated myself to *Single After 50: How to Have the Time of Your Life.*

That night I had a quiet dinner with Annie and Bert, then reviewed my notes. I felt on the brink of something. Before bed, as I brushed my teeth, I yodeled softly.

Why did I still fall asleep crying?

Venturing into downtown San Diego the next day, I found even more water, its lovely bay. I wrote postcards to family and friends describing the sea, the bay, the sun, the sky and the air, all wonderful. Then I bought a t-shirt that said, "San Diego Feels Good All Over." It did indeed!

At their Chamber of Commerce, I collected numerous brochures. With at least thirty-five glossy booklets in hand, I started toward the door, excited. The man behind the desk called out, "Are you going to be here long?" Deliberating for a moment, I turned slowly, then felt goose bumps on my arms as I answered, "Maybe the rest of my life!"

He said, "Welcome," and I threw him a kiss.

Stopping later for a croissant at a coffee house, I perused "Singles Magazine," a guide I found there, listing information about clubs, activities and dating services. It looked interesting, and noting middle-age singles were middle-aged, I laughed to see my yellow leaf of paper flutter happily.

That did it. Fluttering too, I decided to stay. I found a realtor named Turney G. Hitler. Check the phone book, that's his name!

We found a condo I loved, not far from the ocean, with a view of a mountain in the distance. Actually, it was a big hill, but it looked wonderful to me. Everything did.

Several years later, in an article for the *La Jolla Report*, I wrote this about how I chose the area:

After stirring my findings and poring over the results, my big stew began to simmer down. I felt a little like Goldilocks. L.A. was too hot, Florida too old, and La Jolla and San Diego were just right.

How the hell did that ever get published?

But from early on, I knew the wonderful combination of village and city, plus the sheer beauty of both made it the perfect place to begin anew.

I had found my most glorious spot. Now all I needed was to start my new life.

CHAPTER III

HITLER SAVED ME

Speeding to catch up to me in my new world was my old car. I had sent for it immediately, arranging for it to be driven out by someone who answered my ad.

Packed and ready, my Mustang had been sitting patiently just waiting for me to choose our new home.

In Illinois, a month earlier, I'd filled it with kitchen utensils, clothes, precious pictures and semi-precious junk.

As Pam had sat watching me energetically sort piles for garbage, rummage, old home and new home, she said, "Mom, you're acting manicky."

"What's that?" I asked, without looking up. I knew "finicky" but I'd never heard "manicky" before.

"It's a nickname for manic depressive," she replied solemnly.

"P-a-a-m," I retorted in a loud voice, shocked, "I'm fine."

I figured, she's unhappy to see me move and it's bothering her to see me in such good spirits.

But after she left for work I thought about it more. Trusting her judgment as an authority (she was working in a psychiatric unit at Saint Mary's Hospital at the time) I looked up "manic depressive" in *Webster's Dictionary*. The definition read, "referring to a mental disorder characterized by marked emotional shifts from great excitement and high spirits to deep depression - n. one afflicted with this disorder." Damn! Pam was right. I knew I was the "n."

Well, at least I'm having the highs now, as well as the lows, I thought gratefully. It's a step up.

At the airport the next day, Pam said, "Sorry I called you manicky, Mom. Hope I didn't hurt your feelings."

"Pammy darling, you're wonderfully perceptive, and I love you." After we hugged I added with a laugh, "Don't tell anyone at your psych ward your mom's manic depressive, OK?"

She laughed too, and said, "Don't worry, I won't."

We shifted to tears at exactly the same moment, and I boarded my plane.

*****

In La Jolla, ready to start my new life, I was eager for my car to arrive. When it finally drove up to me, I welcomed it to California as I would an old friend. We'd each traveled a long journey and made it. That night, it felt good to have my loyal car parked beside me. Reunited, we were ready to move on.

There was only one problem. We had no place to move.

I had thought once I'd found my condominium, the rest would be simple. But complications developed immediately.

When the landlord discovered my status, an unemployed single woman, he didn't consider me a good risk as a tenant, and refused to sign the lease. Hitler called me to break the news.

I hated having no credibility as a person without a husband! I realized I didn't even possess a credit card in my own name. Tearfully calling Buddy to explain the situation was horrible. I'd felt so proud being independent; now I needed to be taken care of again.

And damn it, Buddy was marvelous. He loved to rescue people, but he was a nice guy, too - the rat! He said calmly, "Francy, tell Hitler to tell the landlord we'll pay six months' rent in advance." Why did I feel part of an awful "B" movie?

We thought the problem was solved, but the landlord, a male chauvinist (we were told by his realtor) still refused me as a tenant, even with the total rent check in hand. We had tried to understand his earlier hesitancy about my being unemployed, but now war was declared.

I felt lucky to have Hitler on my side in this one. He'd been upset before; now he became furious. His forehead grew furrowed, and his already ruddy cheeks flushed crimson. Had he worn a mustache, it would have bristled in anger.

He threatened to take a discrimination charge to REBA, the local real estate board. He began building our case to prepare for battle when we received the news. I was accepted.

The lease was signed by all parties, with Hitler, still belligerent, looking on as a witness. I honestly think he felt disappointed not to have his day in court. He was wonderful.

*****

I made my move with the help of Mario, the new friend I met on the beach. A young man from Cyprus, swarthy and handsome, he was a student at the University of San Diego. On summer break and bored with sunbathing, he made my relocating to La Jolla his special project. After checking my long list of things to do, he jumped up, grinned and shouted, "Avanti!" I think that's Italian for "full speed ahead!"

We drove to a bank and I opened an account.

Next we found an exercise salon where I wrote my first check for a six-month term. It seemed like a life sentence. I wondered if I'd be there that long. Positive that as soon as my thighs were slim and firm, Buddy would want me back, I decided to set the machinery in motion immediately. Mario waited outside for an hour while I worked out.

After lunch we went to companies: furniture, television, the phone and The May. I chose a burnt-orange, plaid couch that reminded me of college, other budget furniture and a television set, all to rent. I felt pushed back in time thirty-five years.

There were so many styles and color choices at Pacific Bell, in consternation I almost ordered a Mickey Mouse phone. At the last minute, I chose plain white, which felt reckless enough. In my former life, I'd been stuck on beige.

At the May Co. I purchased queen-size sheets for my new bed. We had only king size and twin at home, so I'd brought no sheets with me. I didn't want to anyway.

Near the end of the day, I called San Diego Gas & Electric to arrange for hook-up. I still needed to go to the Department of Motor Vehicles and the post office, but they'd have to wait for another time.

I hadn't moved in twenty-five years, and I'd never moved out of state. Amazed at all the essential things to do, I was beginning to realize I'd need more than a gas and electric company to hook up my new life. I felt grateful for Mario's help.

Yet, I didn't want to take advantage of him. Slight but wiry, he insisted on carrying my heavy packages all by himself. Without tiring he'd take me everywhere I needed to go, often waiting patiently while I made difficult decisions - like choosing telephones. But he never complained.

Only once did I see him upset, his nostrils flaring his disapproval. That was when I started to get out of his car before he could open the door for me.

His manners were courtly, his wide grin charming, and his staunch loyalty almost archaic. Every morning he would call early to ask the same question, "Wot we doin' today?"

One morning I said to him, "Mario, I don't know how I could have managed without you. You've been extraordinary and I can't thank you enough. But I feel I should begin doing things for myself. I know my way around a little now, and I'll be OK. I really must learn to be on my own."

"Froncy," (I loved the way he said my name) "if I moved to Illinois, would you help me?"

I said, "Certainly."

Then he added, "If I needed to find my way around, would you show me?"

"Of course I would!"

"Okay then," he said, as if the matter were settled, "so - wot we doin' today?"

I laughed and said, "All right, you asked for it. We're moving in."

I know my Mustang felt relieved as the weight of my possessions was unloaded, and so did I.

The Virgo in me loved getting settled, putting things away and arranging the furniture when it arrived. Small, but modern, with cathedral ceilings in the living room and bedroom, my place was fine for me. Even the orange plaid couch worked with the carpeting. I'd been a little worried.

I glanced around and thought, "Organized chaos, but it's getting better, and almost looking cozy." Then, in the corner by the fireplace, I noticed the empty straw baskets, the first semi-precious junk I'd packed.

Even though Mario had gone home and I was exhausted, I scooped them up and set out to find a nursery. When I discovered one, I filled those baskets and more with lovely California plants, all sizes. Weiba, the owner, who knew everything there was to know about the regional flora, helped me choose them and get them into my car.

When I returned, somehow, feeling like an ant, I managed to get them all out and up to my condominium.

I'd been playing house before, but placing those beautiful plants around inside and on my deck, I realized I had made a home for myself. Unsure whether to laugh or cry, I did both, sitting underneath my new palm tree in the middle of the living room floor.

The next morning when Mario called to ask, "Wot we doin' today?" I said, "Nothing, absolutely nothing. I'm declaring a day of rest."

Then I pulled out the box from beneath my bed labeled "Things to do." In it was the singles magazine I'd found at the coffee house.

I thought of the quote about beginning, and knew the time had come, even for this.

CHAPTER IV

THE COMMUNITY OF THE FORMERLY MARRIED

"Great Expectations," answered the seductive voice at the other end of the phone. The third syllable in "expectations" rose buoyantly, still the voice remained husky. I wondered how the dickens anyone could utter the title of a mid-Victorian novel so sensuously.

"Uh, . . . I'd like to find out more about what you offer . . . or – how you do, uh, what you do. Really, I guess I'd like you to explain what your ad means by . . . 100% access to all members?" The last sentence emerged a squeaky question, and embarrassed, I cleared my throat.

Starting my search for the singles scene, I felt like a country bumpkin struggling to be worldly.

The young woman on the phone seemed to be smiling at my awkwardness as she explained, "We receive many calls from people wishing information. I can assure you Great Expectations is a reputable video dating service. Fulfilling your expectations and engaging relationships are our business."

She sounded programmed.

"I know. I read all that in your ad," I said, unimpressed. Instead of being reassured, I grew skeptical.

"Oh . . . well then, since you've seen our ad, why don't you stop by our office? The best way to find out how we operate is to see for yourself." She was still cordial, but I sensed the smile had faded.

I said, "Maybe I'll do that," but didn't give my name. I dreaded jumping into the singles swirl as much as hopping into my dentist's chair. Would Novocain help? Where should I inject it?

Hoping to speed up the process and get it over with fast, I longed to find someone in ten minutes - to love me, marry me, and take care of me forever. Wouldn't he be fun to show off to Buddy? But with no great expectations for that, I decided against their dating service, at least for then. Besides, I could meet people on my own.

Skimming through "Singles Magazine" the opportunities seemed endless. There were clubs, groups, and activities galore. I could join Singles Sailing, Boating, Golf and Tennis, or try Hiking, Biking, even Scuba Diving. Open for my membership were "Solo," "Aloners" and "Single Phile." I had a warm feeling "The Hug Club" would embrace me, too.

No religious group could be holier than thou. Their singles activities were all listed together.

Many groups specified division by age: 50-plus, 30-plus or young, 20-30ish. I thought it interesting "young" could be stated, yet "middle-age" rarely heard. ("Old" was never even whispered.)

I.Q. was set apart with Mensa for high and Densa for - you guessed it. If you didn't, their membership is still open.

Noticing height requirements for "Tall Singles" I remembered seeing a bumper sticker: TALL SINGLES COME LONGER. Too bad I was only 5'2".

"Let Computer Date Find Your Mate" headlined a big ad.

There were other ads for body building, losing weight, ballroom dancing, foto dating, mixer clubs and self-defense. It seemed a good idea to take self-defense first - to prepare for everything else. I wanted to meet singles, but was beginning to feel overwhelmed.

When would I find time for therapy? Thigh-trimming was still vital, too. I'd need to work in time to work out. Listing everything I wanted to do on my legal pad, I selected from the options according to my priorities.

I attended Singles Golf and Tennis first. They were okay for openers. Then I went to "Lunch Bunch," palatable, and "Happy Talk," dismal discourse.

I returned to some groups, but left others early. I tried almost everything except "Singles Graduates." How could I qualify, just entering singles pre-school?

The "Community of the Formerly Married" at the Lutheran Church was first grade. I learned a lot, mostly sad, but elementary. Programs dealt with adjusting to single life specifically, and readjusting to life in general. The night I went, a divorce counselor spoke, a realistic jolt for me. (I'd only heard a marriage counselor before.) Now, listening to "LIFE AFTER DIVORCE," I shuddered.

After light refreshments a friendship circle formed, everyone's arms around the next person's shoulders. I felt real warmth from that group. Special hugs were given to old friends, new friends and anyone who looked in need. Almost everyone did.

I could see pain on faces, and wondered what mine showed. A woman near me said she could estimate accurately the length of time people had been widowed, divorced or separated just by looking at them. She guessed me as recent.

For the first time, I realized how much men suffered, too. Chatting with Gregory, the man next to me in the friendship circle, I learned he'd started a whole construction company from just one bulldozer, and was proud of his accomplishment. But business success couldn't fill the gaping hole in a world without his wife and children. In his personal life, he felt like a failure.

I talked to several other men and felt sorry for them, unhappy in their small pads, paying alimony and child support. Divorce isn't easy for anyone, and it became a new learning experience to see the hardships and pain from their side.

Later in the evening almost everyone moved on to a private party where a change of mood and purpose became apparent. I noticed hugs growing intimate and pained expressions easing. Soon people began pairing off. It reminded me of a high school party. A "what the hell" attitude began to prevail, and guess who joined in the spirit after a few glasses of wine?!

Gregory, 40-plus, an attractive man with a blond mustache, found me interesting - and I found that interesting. Muscular from working outdoors all his life, he put his huge arm around me carefully, so he wouldn't crush me. We went home together, and among other things, talked all night.

At first "other things" like kissing, holding and touching, seemed a warm extension of the hugging at church, fulfilling that need of reinforcement for us both. As the warmth grew warmer, then hot, it became pure pleasure, passionate and glorious. I hadn't had sex in a long time.

A thrilling addition to my excitement was the idea of having a lover - and a superb one at that. Besides being eager and ardent, he was amazingly punctual, arriving at all the right places at precisely the right time.

The "what the hell" attitude skyrocketed to "screw the world, I want to get off." So I did.

Unfortunately, as the wine wore off, so did my abandon. Horrid feelings of guilt and anguish emerged.

We finished out the night talking about his former wife, and my former person. Buddy and I weren't divorced yet. What else could I call him?

On my deck early the next morning, Greg and I kissed goodbye as a neighbor jogged past, grinning. Suddenly I felt the stereotyped California swinging single who, like the joke, found a meaningful relationship - for the night!

Sitting alone in my bedroom, dejected over a cup of coffee, I forced myself to picture Buddy being with someone else. I held back tears, and quickly shifted again to my indiscretion. Had it been so wrong?

I looked down at the new sheets, rumpled on my bed. After a thoughtful silence, I finally accepted as reality, that dimension of my singlehood. With an audible sigh I rescinded regrets, and allowed myself permission to be a human, sexual woman.

With new motivation I became even more compelled to find someone special, if not to marry, at least for a longer relationship than one night.

I began attending everything, afraid I might miss something - or somebody. To aid my search, I decided to enlist a dating service, and remembering Great Expectations, dropped by their office.

Beth, seductive voice, showed me around and finally answered the question I'd asked on the phone. One hundred percent access to all members wasn't what it implied. It meant you could watch their videotapes, informal interviews conducted by one of the staff. Thinking of my video session soon to be scheduled, my mouth became dry wondering what I'd say. Then the ham in me tried to remember my best angle for the camera.

But written work came first. Filling out a member profile about my background and preferences seemed like an entrance exam. But to what? I felt like an applicant for "The Dating Game." Then I realized with dismay, that's just what I was.

Remembering my journalism courses, I thought of the standard who, what, where, when and why questions. Thinking of myself as the scene of an accident (wasn't I?) I tried putting together pertinent, yet interesting, information about my life.

It wasn't easy.

Confused about the real me, how could I assess myself? I sat as I did in college during a tough final, doodling pensively and gnawing the cuticle on my thumb. Finally I thought of some answers.

Trying to be frivolous, I wrote, "I like to cook and entertain, and even have fun making out the grocery list for a party. I love to travel, too. I never met a place I didn't like."

Becoming serious, I answered another question, in pencil, in case I'd want to change it. "I'd like to live my life with someone who's warm, giving and loving. I want him to be bright and have a marvelous sense of humor."

I left my answer intact, answered other questions and gave my paper to Beth.

On the way home, I imagined this dream man coming into my life. It wasn't so important now to show him off to Buddy. I really hoped to meet him - just for myself.

31

Continuing my furious pace, I added even more activities into my already busy schedule.

I signed up for a course at University of California, San Diego, called "Beyond Divorce." It finally seemed prudent to look in that direction.

Tuesday nights were hectic. Group therapy from 5:15 to 6:45 came just before my class, "How to Manage the Stress in Your Life," from 7-10. I zoomed into the stress class late so regularly, one night the instructor used me as a model . . . of how not to be.

I joined the La Jolla Welcome Wagon Newcomers' Club and met nice ladies. I found Marlene at duplicate bridge, Pat at golf and Naomi at International Club Elite.

It was easy finding lovely women. Interesting, bright, energetic, and savvy females abounded. There were lots of us.

And the men I met?

I didn't feel sorry for all of them. Many were boors who seemed to stand back and be smug, "Here I am, Mr. Wonderful."

Most were looking for one thing.

"I think it's nice to shake hands first," I told several as a joke, but no one laughed. They reminded me of bees trying to buzz every flower, and I began to see the same drones everywhere.

Singles groups made up predominantly of losers, I finally had to admit, were depressing. Often my discouragement became hard to combat, especially when I thought of all those people scurrying everywhere with the sole intention of catching the brass ring - not to mention the wedding band.

I felt sad for them.

I felt even sadder to be one of them.

CHAPTER V

I WENT TO CHURCH AND
BARED MY ASS

God knows I'd been searching everywhere for a miracle. Church was my last hope.

Impressed with stories about an outrageous minister, I decided to attend one of her outstanding sermons. In California, where everything is either outrageous or outstanding, Terry Cole-Whittaker was reputed to be both. I wanted to see for myself.

I'd heard how she generated positive thinking, empowering people to create exactly what they need in this world - like parking places downtown at noon. I felt awe. A parking space downtown at noon is, at the very least, a minor miracle. I could start there and work up.

Sitting front row center I leaned forward, eager to catch her entrance. Would the assistant minister announce, "H-e-e-e-e-r-r-r-e's Terry!"? He didn't. She just paraded in.

Blonde and beautiful, she was the star, radiating energy. With the hoopla of TV cameras grinding, she played to her audience, guilefully using every show biz trick of staging and theatrics. All powerful under the klieg lights, she was the Wizard of Oz.

When she finished dispensing wisdom, heart and courage to her congregation, everyone jumped up in standing ovation.

Mesmerized, I stood, too. Would I really be able to find a place to park?

Filing out after the last hymn, exuberant people, reluctant to leave, congregated outside to visit and chat about the service.

I knew no one, and watching them talk, I felt alone, isolated even in the crowd. Maybe I could meet people if I just relaxed. I smiled at those around me and waited - an anxious orphan hoping to be adopted.

My smile paid off. A lovely young woman, stunning in a gray dress and hat, came up to me and said, "Some of us are going out for lunch. Would you care to join us?"

I wanted to hug her. "Yes, I'd love to."

Smiling and extending her hand, she said, "Good, I'm glad. My name is Carlette. We're going to The Swallows - is that a problem for you?"

"Hi, I'm Francy, and there's no problem. It sounds like a fun place. Eat ... swallow ... 'The Swallows.' Cute name for a restaurant, right?"

Her face said "wrong."

First on one foot, then the other, Carlette began, "Well, uh, there's something you ought to know. They do have food, and we can have lunch there, but ... it's not a restaurant."

"Oh really? What is it then?" I asked, picturing some sort of quaint mission like Capistrano, famous for swallows.

"It's a ... a ... nudist colony." She glanced at me to check my reaction. Seeing me stunned, but still standing, she brightened and continued, "It's an interesting experience Francy, and I'm sure you'll enjoy it."

Before I could respond, a couple who'd been standing nearby approached. "I'm Phil and this is Ellie," the man said. "We heard Carlette and she's right, you know."

Ellie added her own "Hello," and "we hope you come along to see for yourself."

From behind Carlette a handsome man appeared with a pert youngster, her face a replica of his.

"I'm Jim," he said, "and this is my daughter, Kelly. It would be nice to have you join us. Kelly's ten and will be coming along, too."

My consternation obvious, Kelly shot over a look of encouragement to me as if to say, "It's easy. Even a child can do it."

I returned a wan smile. But looking at her longer, I began to grin. As I watched that cute, spunky kid, I saw myself at that age. A real daredevil, I used to love to dive off the high board at the pool and ride my bike full speed with no hands,.

Even now I'm considered gutsy by my friends. But this is ridiculous, I thought, as I envisioned being nude with people I scarcely knew. Would it be easier with people I knew well? My grin broadened.

I imagined the next phone conversation with my mother.

"Hi, Mom. How are you?"

"Fine, dear. Anything new?"

"Nothing much ... Oh, I met some lovely people after church on Sunday, and we all went out for lunch together."

"That's nice. Where did you go?"

"To a nudist colony. The food was great!"

An absurd scenario, but with Mom in the picture, my grin disappeared.

I sputtered to the group, "I'm sorry, I can't ... I just couldn't ... I mean, there's no way I would. Thanks for asking me. I'm flattered, but ... "

Ellie interrupted. "Don't you want to go to a nudist colony?"

"Oh yes, of course, I do. It's been on my list of things to do for some time now. I've just never gotten around to it. You know, Illinois doesn't have any - at least I don't think so. Anyhow not where I lived. So ... someday I want to do that for sure. But ... just not today." I certainly hoped she didn't think me a prude.

"Why *not* today?" Phil asked, persistent.

I answered in a low voice, "I don't know," and realized it was true.

As I thought about it more, with everyone's eyes focused on me, and all that California sunshine warm on my head - somehow my going began to grow plausible.

It struck me that no one from my former life need ever find out. And unknown in San Diego, my anonymity felt like a safe, protective shield. Lonely isolation was beginning to feel more like comfortable privacy.

Something else I liked - I wasn't there in the role of anyone's daughter, sister, wife or mother. It felt good to be my own private organization, "Myself Anonymous."

I realized with mounting excitement that by now, my going to a nudist colony for lunch, straight from church that very day, had advanced from plausible ... to perfectly logical.

But why had my hands turned so cold? And why was I furiously biting the inside of my cheek ... both of them? How could I go when I felt so scared?

I found a way. I reached back in time and once more became the little girl I used to be on the high board, poised and ready to dive off. She gave me the courage I needed.

Excited, I knocked off Carlette's hat as I hugged her. Laughing, I swooped it up with one hand, grabbed Kelly with the other and said, "Let's go!"

You'd think I'd said, "Lift off." Enthusiastic shouts came from everyone, excited and happy now that all systems were go.

"Great, I'm delighted," said Carlette, catching her hat in mid-air from my toss.

"Hey, she's going!" Ellie announced.

Kelly squeezed my hand and grinned to the others, "I knew she would."

Jim volunteered to get his station wagon.

As we all climbed in, I remembered. Visiting a nudist colony really was on my list of things to do someday - granted, pretty far down.

"I forget, Daddy, how long does it take?" Kelly asked, the usual child's question at the start of a trip.

"Not long, honey, about an hour." Jim answered.

Everyone was eager to get there. Well, almost everyone. The minute my door had slammed shut, I wanted to shove it open and jump out. Too embarrassed, I sat frozen to my seat, perspiration dewy above my upper lip. I pictured the See's candy on my coffee table at home. During moments of extreme anxiety I crave a chocolate connection. Right then, I could have eaten the whole box!

On the way, I listened solemnly to the excited chatter of the others. In a festive mood, they were acting as if they were off to a marvelous party.

Did they have parties there? My mind wandered to possible invitations they could send:

PLEASE COME
DRESS: CASUAL
or
COME AS YOU ARE
BLACK TIE became hilarious as I envisioned that as the total dress. What would the women wear, pearls?

I thought of some of the black-tie parties I'd attended and, picturing them that way, laughed out loud.

"Are you all right?" asked Carlette.

"Yes," I replied, but my laughter trailed off.

"You'll love it," Ellie said, trying to be reassuring.

Why was I doubtful?

Jim, from the driver's seat, threw back, "The free feeling is wonderful."

Why should I feel captive?

With closed eyes, Kelly rubbed her hands slowly over her arms and shoulders. "The water feels s-o-o-o silky when you're swimming."

Just ready to say, "I can't go, I didn't bring my suit," I realized I didn't need one.

Why did I feel terror?

The trip I'd thought interminable ended too soon. We were there.

Reluctant to get out, I said, "I think I'll just stay here in the station wagon and read." (I'd suddenly remembered I hadn't shaved my legs for several days.)

"Read what ... the church bulletin?" Jim asked. Everyone laughed and pulled me along.

"Which way to the dressing rooms ... or maybe I should say undressing rooms?" I asked, a feeble attempt at humor.

"There are none," said Carlette. "We just get out of our clothes right here."

Oh my God, how can I? I began wheezing - and I'm not asthmatic. Perched alone now on my imagined high diving board, I wanted desperately to climb down the ladder and go home. Damn! Where's that spunky kid I used to be?

Kelly must have sensed my need for a ten-year-old. She looked at me with compassion and took my hand, pulling me away from the others. I followed, paraphrasing a quote from the Bible: "And a little child shall lead me."

We undressed in silence, back to back. It was awful taking my clothes off. Ye gads - it was broad daylight!

With my heart pounding, I unlayered as slowly as I could. When my shaking fingers unbuttoned the last button on my blouse, I panicked. Why hadn't I worn a sweater, vest and coat, too? Then I remembered. It was summer.

When I got down to the bottom line, I turned uneasily to look around. I couldn't see the others, but noticed Kelly, already nude, waiting for me.

The stubble on my legs looked thick, but - what the hell, I thought with abandon. I slipped out of my bra and pants and flung them to the ground. Then giggling nervously, Kelly and I made our way together through the gates, stark naked, no one even bothering to notice.

The nonchalance of those inside helped diminish my terror. Being nude with others can be compared to jumping into icy water. If you think about it, it sounds dreadful. If you stick one toe in, it's worse. But if you plunge in (or you're pushed in) all at once, after the initial shock, it almost feels good. I said almost. I could have "chugalugged" a can of Hershey's syrup.

The first people we saw were playing tennis (mixed doubles) wearing sweat bands, tennis shoes and socks. The standard garb for the game only made the scene more ludicrous. It was their entire attire.

A fascinated spectator, I watched, the way you watch tennis, eyes moving laterally to follow the action. I can tell you with authority, the real action of that game dropped lower than usual. Besides noticing how unevenly matched the players were, I asked myself, "WHAT IN THE HELL AM I DOING HERE?"

It's not an ordinary script, you know:

MAIN CHARACTER: *Naïve lady from Illinois.*
SETTING: *Nudist colony in southern California.*
ACTION: *Walking around in the buff after church on Sunday.*
THEME: *Experiencing the experience is a wonderful experience.*
PLOT: *None.*

Maybe it could be a book someday, I thought, as I watched the bizarre tennis game. It would surely be funnier than the current soggy saga of my life.

We hadn't seen the rest of our group inside yet, and Kelly had gone off to find her Dad. Thinking about seeing them - I mean "see" in the Biblical sense -- I began to feel awkward and embarrassed.

It hadn't been so bad with total strangers; I'd felt an observer. And it had been OK with Kelly; she hadn't reached puberty yet. But now, at the thought of being a participant in nudism with people I knew, I yearned for a fig leaf - or three!

Weird questions began racing through my mind. What would Carlette look like under her grey dress and hat? Would Ellie be blonde all over? Should I look directly at Jim and Phil below the belt? ... what belt? ... or glance at them casually? Would their penises be large or small? Erect? How could they not be, with pretty women around? Oh God, they were walking toward me!

Shy at first, I looked away. Then, coy, I looked down. They were near me now. I could see their toes. Beginning feet first, I moved up until, finally, blatantly, I looked at them all.

Carlette was beautiful; Ellie, brunette; and Jim's and Phil's penises were average and behaving themselves. (I'd looked directly.)

39

Jim and Phil looked at me, too, and somehow it was all right. I thought of some of the awful men I'd seen at bars who could undress you with their leering eyes. Here, at least, there were no mixed messages. And with the openness, the lewdness was gone. We were all human beings reduced to the same basic uniform.

The inhabitants, men, women and children, relaxed and tan all over, seemed happy and comfortable with their life-style, their nudity natural, not shameful.

In the woodsy, camp-like atmosphere, laughing children were being swung by their parents in the playground. A grandfather and his grandson played Ping-Pong with an easy banter and warmth between them. The element of family togetherness added a wholesome quality.

A swimming pool, sauna and Jacuzzi were on the premises for people to enjoy, as well as a clubhouse open to all. And, oh yes, we found the dining room, informal with wooden tables and benches.

Suddenly ravenous, we all went inside and sat down, taking extreme caution to guard against splinters. The food looked appetizing, but I hopped up - carefully - and headed straight for the machines by the door. Playing them like the slots, I cranked out three candy bars fast. For my entrée, I ordered a hot fudge sundae, double chocolate and heavy on the syrup. I skipped dessert.

The waitresses were nudists, but wore aprons with bibs for protection which, oddly enough, created a rather sexy effect. In a forward flash, I pictured myself dressed like that, hostess at a candlelit supper for two. I had the perfect apron in mind, a little French number made of black eyelet piqué. My elusive dream man didn't know what he was missing!

Going swimming felt great. I hadn't been skinny-dipping since I was a kid at camp. Gliding along in a sidekick, I called out to Kelly, "You're right, the water does feel silky, and I love it."

As I climbed up the ladder to get out of the pool, I started to tug at my suit to pull it down, when I realized - no suit! I got out laughing and brazenly stretched my arms skyward. I threw back my head and seeing the clear blue above, uttered, "Yea, God!" I knew then what Jim had meant when he'd said, "The free feeling is wonderful."

Later in the afternoon, when the trees began blocking out the sunshine, Kelly said, "I'm getting cold but I hate to go." Everyone felt the same reluctance to leave.

Unconsciously, we may have gone as voyeurs to see an X-rated production, but ended up bit players in a scene rated PG. Nudists together for a few short hours, we felt a sense of comradery in the shared experience.

On the quiet trip back, gazing at the pink and orange sky highlighting the sunset, I reflected on the day. Had it all really happened? It must have, because being dressed now felt odd, like walking on land after being on a ship.

Closing my eyes, I thought back to the morning church service. The sermon had covered more ground than just parking places.

"If your life isn't working, move on," Terry had said. Well, I'd certainly done that. But instead of moving forward, I'd been racing nowhere. Thank God I'd fallen off my bike!

I sat up to watch the sun disappear, and contemplated the main message. "If a relationship isn't right for you, let go. Create what you need to transform your life."

For the first time since the separation, that began to seem possible. Coming to grips with baggage I'd been lugging around too long, I finally let go of anger, hurt, despair - and Buddy. Of course, it wasn't total, but it was a miraculous beginning. The thought of my struggle easing brought me new peace and permission to slow down.

I felt light, unburdened and released. And the free feeling, like skinny-dipping, was wonderful.

CHAPTER VI

REBIRTHING IN A HOT TUB
– AT WOMB TEMPERATURE

You won't believe it. I didn't either. Downtown at noon I found a parking place. There it was, a wide open space just waiting for me. It was nowhere near my destination, but that didn't matter; the walk was exhilarating! With my new positive attitude, I refused to be daunted.

Since that incredible day, I'd journeyed from Oz to Never Never Land. I kept right on traveling, moving forward and progressing well.

I'd pared my frenzied pace, but, "The purpose of life, after all, is to live it - to taste experience to the utmost, to reach out eagerly and without fear for newer and richer experiences." After reading Eleanor Roosevelt's words, I jotted them down and posted them eye-level on my refrigerator.

Earlier I'd heard about a process called Rebirthing, but had dismissed it as "California kookie." Now, with Eleanor's credo my new domestic policy, I elected "to taste experience to the utmost."

At the World Healing Center in Solana Beach, I studied their brochure and discovered that Rebirthing is a powerful technique which permits people to open up and feel life more abundantly. Often the process takes them back to their birth experience, and is accomplished by deep breathing and affirmations (positive thoughts). I didn't fully understand, but read on.

"The quality of our thoughts determines the quality of our life." Rebirthing allows negative thinking, plus painful memories lodged in our subconscious to surface and release. My thoughts had become positive on the conscious level now, but I knew, subconsciously, they could still use help.

There are two methods of Rebirthing, dry and wet. For the dry form, you lie down in the presence of a rebirther, who launches you into a breathing pattern. The wet method begins in a hot tub (at womb temperature) with a snorkel and nose plugs.

With my penchant for plunging, I chose the wet way and, after completing proper arrangements, jumped in.

Being held down, even though gently, by my trained rebirther was horrid, and I hated it. Unlike room temperature, womb temperature was hot and uncomfortable. I struggled to get out and get on with it, eager for the process to begin.

Lynn, my rebirther (young enough to be my daughter), told me she'd rarely seen anyone so impatient to be born. My mother verified that, when I checked with her later.

Emerging from the hot tub, my only feeling was one of relief. After following Lynn to the mats, we lay quietly side by side, where I felt nothing - except irritation that I felt nothing.

What was supposed to happen? And when?

Lynn whispered, "Breathe deeper," then demonstrated how. "And begin your affirmations," she reminded me.

As I followed her instructions, my skin began to tingle; tenseness disappeared. An odd duo of aliveness and relaxation seemed to penetrate, then permeate my body. Soon after, I experienced Rebirthing.

For me it had nothing to do with going through the birth canal, although I understood sometimes people do feel that.

What I sensed was an amazing perception of the happiness of my mother and father at my birth. I saw my mother smiling, her head on a pillow. In pictures of her circa that era, she'd always worn her dark hair arranged in a bun. Now it was loose and flowing on the white pillowcase. With her blue eyes shining and her cheeks flushed, she looked radiant. My father, beaming too, stood beside her, holding her hand.

My parents already had a son and a daughter, so it hadn't mattered to them what sex I was. As a child, whenever I used to hear that, I'd thought of it as indifference, and not caring.

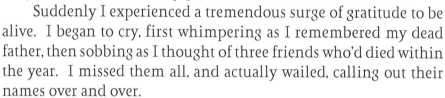

Now I understood it as total acceptance and love. They wanted whatever they got - me!

Suddenly I experienced a tremendous surge of gratitude to be alive. I began to cry, first whimpering as I remembered my dead father, then sobbing as I thought of three friends who'd died within the year. I missed them all, and actually wailed, calling out their names over and over.

I began to feel overwhelmed with what a special gift life is, and how lucky I was to have it. Never before had I acknowledged it as so miraculous, or with such appreciation.

Oddly then, as if from another world, I heard myself uttering, "Thank you, Buddy," again and again. Somehow I felt rebirthed from him, or by him, I wasn't sure which. It was all confused and strange. But I remember being grateful for his pushing me out (delivering me?), forcing me to create my new life.

For the first time, I perceived it as no accident or mistake, but destined. I relished the sense of completion.

After lying quietly for a time, my thoughts evolved to what I wanted to do with my precious life now that I appreciated its value.

I decided to accelerate my personal growth. What was my potential? I had no idea - but I felt like pushing.

I set goals for myself - high, yet achievable. I'd need to become more centered, less scattered. More focused, less fragmented. I could do it. The clarity of purpose was a brilliant beam of light showing me the way.

Enveloped in the glow, I sensed another curious combination, power and peace. Usually with power one thinks of boldness, drive - ambition. Conquest or control.

Now I viewed power as energy, a dynamic force and strength. And the control was mine, over myself. As I understood that, a lovely sense of peace emerged.

Extraordinary. The whole experience was extraordinary.

Without moving, Lynn and I began to talk quietly. "Rebirthing varies with each individual," she told me. Before she'd been rebirthed, she always felt that she "should be somewhere else, doing something different. Never satisfied."

I listened, trying hard to picture her as anything other than placid and serene.

She went on, "Scattered energy makes it difficult to accomplish anything, or to know yourself. Focus and clarity are good and give you a sense of your own power."

I nodded in agreement, understanding now from my own experience.

Before leaving, I asked why my process had begun so late. She answered, "It started in the hot tub. You just didn't realize it."

I hugged Lynn goodbye, feeling I'd known her all my life. In a way - I guess I did.

*****

Acting on my decision to accelerate my personal growth, I signed up for more courses. But instead of choosing those geared to stress and divorce, I let out my clutch and relaxed.

Using the University of California San Diego Extension Catalogue, "Explore," as a guide, I chose the new path I wanted to follow: enrichment.

I took a symphony class and art appreciation. I even tried a course called "Release the Writer Within You." Could it be possible one was bottled up inside?

Exploring by myself, off campus, I took a side trip around the area. I drove through the mountains scouting out little-known places and hard-to-get-to spots. The rarefied air smelled piney and fresh, and suddenly it struck me, I'd developed an intense awareness of odors, textures and colors. In the valleys, the orange blossoms were an unusual fragrance to me. I drew up close to sniff their sweetness. When I came upon the desert in spectacular bloom, I realized I'd never before seen a cactus flower outside of a dime store. Borrego Springs offered a less stifled selection.

I loved the loud, brilliant blossoms shouting out to be heard. Although common, they hobnobbed unabashedly with royalty, those majestic purple blooms that commanded my attention in regal fashion.

I obeyed with pleasure.

Then, amidst their radiant splendor, I plopped down on a bench, sprawled out with my face to the sun, opened up to life's abundance and blossomed, too.

On the trip back, still elated, I noticed the pale green leaves bursting forth on the deciduous trees, and stopped to examine their ridges, delicate, yet strong. I identified with them, feeling like a new shoot myself.

I began to see a profusion of yellow everywhere. Witnessing for the first time the wild mustard resplendent on the hills, I swallowed hard, on the verge of tears.

When I arrived home, and saw my purple plum tree an explosion of pink on my deck, I cried aloud.

Spring had come to California, and I was reborn.

CHAPTER VII

CALIFORNIA GROWS ON ME

"For men and women who have accepted the reality of change, the need for endless learning and trying is a way of living, a way of thinking, a way of being awake and ready."

John Gardner
Self-Renewal – The Individual
and the Innovative Society

After coming alive again, the next order of progression was to GROW - so I joined. The acronym stands for "The Giving and Receiving Organization for Women."

At a seven o'clock breakfast meeting, I brushed the sleep out of my eyes, and met women who were wide-awake, ready and all set to grow!

Part of the process was "networking": sharing ideas, information and resources. The term was used as a verb, and the action included standing up to tell briefly about yourself and your job.

"Sharing," as it's called, that first time, was scary. With clammy hands, and a frog in my throat, I introduced myself. Then I said, "At the end of a long marriage I moved here to begin a new life. My first full-time job was getting my head on straight."

Placing one hand firmly under my chin, and the other hand at the top of my noggin, I demonstrated, by an exaggerated twist into place, that the job was accomplished. It felt good to be able to joke about it, and we all laughed together with mutual understanding.

Feeling the support of the group, I went on – a bit braver,, "Now, I'm the advertising manager of a small newspaper, 'The *La Jolla Report.*' The only one selling ads, I can claim the title."

People laughed again, and someone from the group called out, "Sure...go for it!"

After giving a mini job description (and a minor ad hustle) I finished by saying, "This is a great group, and I'm happy to be here."

As I sat down, everyone applauded, and I felt wonderful.

Applause is many hands patting you on the back, causing you to sit up straight instead of slump. Everyone sat erect at GROW.

Rising next, the young lady to my right, so effervescent she bubbled over, spouted out, "Hi, I'm Helice, founder and president of the Difference Makers." She waited for people to reply, "Hi."

"I believe everyone in this world is important!" Enthusiastic comments around the room agreed.

She continued, "After pinning ribbons with the words, 'Who I am Makes a Difference' on people, and giving them upbeat messages while doing it, I discovered they began feeling better about themselves. So - I started pinning ribbons on everyone I saw, wherever I went." She paused, delighted as people clapped their approval.

I didn't join in the applause. The idea seemed preposterous, and I thought, "This woman is wacko."

She went on, "I started promoting the concept. Now endorsed by the city council, it's accepted and done within the school system, throughout big corporations and by senior citizens."

Her credibility increased, but it was still hard to believe. She looked like a kid, with her buck teeth spaced apart and a grin so wide it crinkled her eyes shut.

Reading from her brochure, she quoted Spencer Johnson, co-author of *The One Minute Manager*, "Receiving recognition with the 'Who I am Makes a Difference' ribbon is both fun and extremely important. The Difference Makers have created a necessary vehicle which will bring about a great change in our society." I had to admit, that sounded impressive.

As I looked up at her, she spontaneously pulled me to my feet and asked if I'd accept a ribbon from her.

What could I say but, "Yes"?

With her quick grin slowed down so I could see her eyes, she said, "Francy, I can tell you're a special woman. You've come a long way, all by yourself, and you've created the new life you wanted."

Becoming solemn, she added, "This ribbon is to remind you of your excellence and your significance to the world. I hope you will think often about how important you are." Then she hugged me and grinned, and her eyes crinkled shut again.

Hugging her back, I felt like the overnight star of a smash hit play. I hadn't received a mere snip of ribbon; I'd become the honored recipient of a Tony Award! It was hokey - but who cared? Feeling important felt terrific. This time I led her applause.

Mary, a subdued, soft-spoken contrast to Helice, had just as much drive in her elegant way. Speaking out against the fashion industry's apparent disregard for women in mid-life, she asked, "Why do they neglect us? Why can't they produce good-looking clothes that aren't dowdy? And in sensible sizes?" Adamant, she credited "Toastmasters" for helping her voice control.

A stunning, white-haired (just the right size of portly) middle-aged fashion model, she'd developed "The Ageless Woman Concept or How to Accept Middle-Essence," and was presenting workshops on the subject.

Other GROW members were involved in her project.

Cecile, young, vivacious, black and beautiful, got up with a bounce. "I'm president and owner of 'Body Moves Workout Program' and I handle the exercise and fitness portion of Mary's workshop."

She pointed to Sharon across the room, "See that gorgeous blonde in the beige suit, pink blouse and perfect eye make-up? She's owner and director of 'Rainbows by Sharon' and is the cosmetic and color expert of our team."

Sharon rose to explain how the three of them had met at

GROW and decided to merge their talents. She announced, "Our workshop is now listed in 'Access to Learning,' a national adult education program." I felt proud of them all, and began to realize what important results can come from networking.

I listened with interest to everyone who spoke.

There were professional women: a dentist, a lawyer and several therapists. I remembered back to the days (not long ago) when, if a woman was a professional, she was a teacher or a nurse.

Several of the women had started their own businesses on shoestrings - made of guts. One of them was Fay.

Divorced and left with seven minor children, she went back to school to learn how to support her family. She decided to look into what she knew best, managing a household.

"My Phi Beta Kappa brother was the math genius," she told us, "but I studied marketing and promotion, and learned how to figure, too."

"Now I'm the owner of 'Auntie Fay, Inc. Agency,' a domestic placement service staffed with maids, cooks, chauffeurs and housekeepers. And I'm opening a 'White Glove Maintenance Service' for businesses soon." She received a huge ovation.

Patt Parkins and Marcia Hootman, co-authors of *How to Forgive Your Ex-husband (and Get On With Your Life)* held my rapt attention.

Patt related the major premise of the book: "Unforgiving attitudes held by many divorced people can affect the quality of their lives. Facing up to these often-repressed feelings is the only way to achieve a healthier, happier future."

The room became still as many grew thoughtful. Was she right? I chose to look down rather than face up. I had just barely made it to "acceptance." How could I progress to "forgiveness" so fast? Christ, I was no saint!

To the roomful of quiet listeners Marcia added, "We found that shedding the anger and need for revenge frees women to explore new directions. As women focus on getting on with their lives, they're less focused on 'getting back' at their ex-husbands."

Their book was selling well. I guess many women wanted to forgive their ex-husbands, but needed a "how-to" book to do it.

The noise level in the room returned to normal when Patt and Marcia announced they were buying new clothes and make-up for their appearance on "Donahue."

Not everyone in GROW was successful. Some were in transition, bravely changing jobs or occupations they'd had for years. Bored or dissatisfied, not working up to their potential, they wanted to do something different, or try for something better. Even in mid-life.

Leads for business opportunities were asked for and given; roommates were requested and garage sales announced. These women received the total support of the group. Everyone admired their courage, and the applause given to them was just as resounding as it was for those who'd made it big.

Even when one woman dejectedly announced she'd lost the job she needed and loved, I was amazed to hear cheering and shouts of encouragement like, "Great! Now you can move on to something better."

The last people to share were Sondra and Jean. Both were promoting Anthony Robbins, the man who turns fear into power by "The Firewalk Experience". I remembered seeing him on the Merv Griffin Show.

"He and others have walked barefoot unharmed across a bed of red-hot coals," said Sondra, her face glowing with excitement, I wondered if her feet had blisters.

Jean reported, "It's incredible. Our limiting belief systems can be overcome by N.L.P., neurolinguistic programming. 'Psychology Today' called it the most powerful vehicle for change in existence." As she paused for a sip of water, I watched closely, expecting steam to escape.

Together they invited us all to Del Mar, La Jolla's northern neighbor, to view a firewalk video, take a seminar of instruction and walk across burning coals.

The room began to buzz with controversial discussion. Everyone was curious. Most were hesitant; a few planned to go.

Without even checking my calendar, I knew I had a conflict.

We were still chatting noisily about the Firewalk Experience when the facilitator began to introduce the speaker.

"GROW programs are planned to make us feel alive, green and growing," she said. Today, Audrey, a clinical psychologist will discuss goal setting.

I took notes: "Decide what it is you want to do. Be specific," she emphasized. "Figure out what you're willing to give to accomplish it. Decide what you're willing to *give up* to achieve it. Set your priorities daily to allow for it. Then do it!"

"Short-term, intermediate and long-range goals should be established, and written down," she continued.

"Your supreme goal is valuable to know. Go for it; but guard against obsession. Whimsical gleams can be entered, too. They're fun. Learn to smell the roses, and recharge. Only you can choose the proper balance for yourself."

She concluded by having us fill out columns headed by "I Love To Do," and "My Perfect Scene," to help us realize what makes us happiest. "Write down what it is you want for yourself, too. And don't be afraid to ask for it," she said.

Putting all that in writing made life amazingly clear. Somehow - on paper - my world seemed less burdensome and stodgy.

I added some gleams to my heavy-duty goals and lightened up.

My short-term goal was to read *How to Forgive Your Ex-Husband,* and study up on Joan of Arc.

My intermediate goal was to learn all I could about writing. ("I love to write" was at the top of my "Love To Do" list.)

My long-range goal was to forgive and forget, then write a book about how noble I was.

My supreme goal was to smell the roses and be happy.

After I finished writing everything down, I read it over.

"My Perfect Scene" was perfect. On paper.

CHAPTER VIII

DR. DAN

I left GROW clutching new goals and gleams. I also had the firewalk brochure tucked under my arm.

Damn! Why did I feel compelled to investigate everything? Would my metamorphosis never change? I wanted to laugh, but it wasn't funny. Or was it?

*****

Dan Kiley would have roared. (In Illinois I used to complain to him about my dull life.) I wished we could rap together about my California adventures. I missed him.

Psychologist, and now noted author of *The Peter Pan Syndrome*, he'd been just "Dr. Dan" to the juveniles he counseled at the Adolph Myer Zone Center in Decatur, Illinois.

He was good. His record there for recidivism was outstanding, the lowest in the state.

His record for that with me was lousy. I returned to him often.

I went with problems I wanted to air out. Nothing hyperventilating - just normal stuff.

"What is normal?" I asked him once, trying to understand myself better.

That massive man, 6'4" tall, with thick, shaggy gray hair, and

a mustache that merged with his goatee, put down his Mickey Mouse phone, glanced at his Mickey Mouse watch and grinned, "Who knows?"

Our first session had been after my dad died. His death was the first real adversity in my life and I wasn't handling it well. Besides experiencing my loss and seeing my mother alone, I felt scared, one rung closer to death myself.

I always got dramatic about moving on in life. At 12, when I began menstruation at camp, I cried to my friend, Elaine, "God, I'm a woman, now. Before you know it, I'll get married, have babies, be a grandmother – and die!" I pictured myself old and withered, rigid in my coffin, and shivered. Morose from the fast-forward projection of my life and demise, it took me three hours to emerge from under the olive-drab blanket on my bunk.

But Dad's death was tragic reality. I spent a whole winter reading Kierkegaard and Sartre, lost in existential depression.

When I finally got myself to Dan, he advised, "Feel your pain; don't submerge it. Get away alone. Cry. Scream! Rant and rave like a maniac. For ten minutes. Maybe fifteen, if it really feels good. Be sure to set a time limit. Don't wallow in your grief. Allow it, and then move on." I was sorry I hadn't gone to him sooner.

When I got home, I headed straight for the woods next to my house. I wanted to let go, as Dan had suggested, but instead, sat stony, unable to cry.

Somberly, I reflected on moments with my dad. Did he know I loved him?...I hadn't told him enough...why not?...I should have... Dad, I love you..."DADDY!" I screamed, and furious outrage surged forth. "How dare you abandon me? How dare you leave my poor mother alone?!"

I stomped my feet in anger and fell back on the ground. I flailed my arms at my sides and kicked my heels hard into the soft, spring earth. I was a monstrous two-year-old having a full-blown tantrum, even managing to get muddied up in the process.

After it was over, my throat hurt, my eyes stung and my shoes were ruined, yet I felt better. I sat up and looked at my watch. Seventeen minutes had passed. I'd splurged - but it was worth it. For the first time since my dad's death in October, I forgave him for dying.

I padded into my house in my stocking feet, after dropping my shoes (clods of mud) on the welcome mat. I hugged my kids, took a warm bath and fixed dinner. The girls asked no questions, just seemed relieved to see me responsive again. Watching me at dinner, Buddy breathed more easily, too.

That night in bed, Buddy and I talked for hours about high school, college days, the war, our children, life - and death. When we made love, it was with the same wild passion as in younger days. But added was the special tenderness of our years together.

After Buddy went to sleep, I cried softly for ten minutes (timing it on the clock's luminous dial in the darkness) then fell asleep, too.

The next morning I looked out our bedroom window to the woods below and decided, whenever I felt the need to unwind, I'd go there.

CHAPTER IX

ON TA, TM, ME

While living in Illinois, besides seeing Dan Kiley, I began to look for other methods of opening up. I yearned for the "white light" - illumination and life *before* death.

After reading Eric Berne's, *Games People Play* and Thomas Harris', *I'm OK, You're OK,* I got our whole family involved with Transactional Analysis (TA). TA had become faddish; many people were latching on to it. But it worked for us, and our family interaction improved.

TA's main premise: within each of us is a parent, adult and child, with variations in each category. If your husband asks, "Do you know where my cufflinks are?" you can lecture from your critical parent, "If you'd put them where they belonged, they wouldn't be lost."

The adaptive child within you might respond, "You're always losing things. Find them yourself."

An adult transaction would be, "I haven't seen them, but I'll help you search."

The cufflink story is good for illustration, but it reminds me of learning French. "La plume de ma tante" doesn't come up much in conversation. Buddy didn't wear cufflinks, either.

Still, we learned a lot. Everyone began to "come on straight" with one another, not in detrimental fashion, but in healthy, caring ways. Our house rules became "open communication" instead of "family hold back."

Being rational in our adult computers was steady and reliable, but sometimes boring. The "natural child" was lots more fun.

We loved that carefree state where you could act playful, be spontaneous - and giggle. Buddy was the only one who found it difficult to shed his "adult" computer. After much prompting and coaching from the rest of us, he got into his "kid" role at times, but still had trouble playing it convincingly.

I was in my "natural child" so often that Peggy, then ten, delighted in chiding me, "C'mom Mom, get in your 'adult'!" With a big grin on Mother's Day, she gave me the book, *I'm OK. You're Not So Hot.* It was one of my best presents.

After TA came TM, Transcendental Meditation. Marcy became involved with it when she went to the University of Missouri, and strongly urged the rest of us to try it. Her new friend, Rick, recommended it, too.

One night, five of us trooped together through a snowstorm to hear an introductory lecture. We comprised the bulk of the audience.

Mystical gobbledy-gook about levels of consciousness, life's supreme values, ultimate states of experience, sap that brings changes and the horizon that becomes bigger as you climb higher up the mountain were all related with dispassionate serenity by a woman with no chin. Amy and Pam never went back.

Buddy, Peggy and I forged ahead to the next phase, individual sessions.

When I went to mine, I opened the door to a small room, where Indian incense hung heavy in the air. Soft sitar music was playing on a record player somewhere, obviously out of sight. The lute-like music might have been soothing had the record not been scratched.

The woman with no chin appeared out of nowhere and ushered me into a stall-like area set off by silk curtains. I felt like I was in a plush voting booth. But the only campaign poster in that inner sanctum was a portrait of the highly revered Maharishi Mahesh Yogi, the founder and head guru of TM. Beneath his picture was a tiny table covered with a doily, either ecru or soiled. Lit candles and a vase of flowers were set on top of it.

Part of the ritual, we'd been told, was for each person to bring a fresh flower and a new, white linen handkerchief to present as gifts to the Maharishi. Just as I was about to place my offerings on the table, I sneezed - right into the handkerchief! Dear God. What was I to do? I couldn't leave dirty linen as a present.

Embarrassed, and perplexed about proper procedure, I looked up at the Maharishi's face on the wall. His penetrating eyes peered out at me from beneath cascades of streaming hair, and that gentle soul seemed to say, "It's OK. I don't need your hanky. Cut through this bullshit and go learn about TM."

I deposited the flower on the doily, stuffed the handkerchief into my pocket and walked back into the outer room, where the woman asked simply, "Now that the perfunctories are over, would you like to learn how to meditate?"

She gave me a mantra, a made-up word with no meaning. "This is your very own, personal sound, especially created to fit your unique personality," she said. "No one else has it. You are to tell it to no one - ever. If you do, it could interfere with your concentration."

I clamped my jaw tightly and promised myself I'd never breathe it to a living soul.

Her instructions went on. Repeat your mantra silently without straining, to get your mind drifting off into nothingness. Sit relaxed with your eyes closed; but don't go to sleep. Keep your arms and legs uncrossed, your hands loose in your lap. Let your head fall forward. Remember; think your mantra again and again, again and again, again and again.

It happened! I experienced it. I went into a trance-like reverie - a blankness, a nothingness. A complete rest.

Afterward, I felt refreshed and exhilarated. I started to get up quickly to go home and tell the family, but was cautioned, "Sit quietly for another five minutes. Rouse yourself gently. If you come out of meditation too fast, you may get a headache."

She told me to perform the same procedure at home, twice daily, twenty minutes at a time. Then I was to come back for another few sessions, to be checked.

I loved TM, and kept it up for several years. I looked forward to my quiet time alone when I could block out worldly pressures and feel at peace. Upon awakening from it, I felt rested, refreshed and better equipped to handle my busy life. One of my New Year's resolutions (every year) is to get back to it.

Peggy loved TM, too, and it has become an integral part of her life. She, Marcy and Rick "med" every day even now.

Buddy practiced it a short time. He tricked me into telling him my mantra (how could he?!) and then insisted it was the same as his. We laughed about it, but he said the credibility was gone for him.

I said, "What a cop-out," but he never meditated again. He seemed glad for the excuse not to.

*****

When Buddy began chain-smoking, I should have known something was wrong. He didn't smoke.

During every argument - and there were more and more - he began to talk about divorce.

I reacted calmly, of course, by screaming, "No, no - NO!" Divorce was the worst thing in life I could think of.

A close friend told me about Marriage Encounter. I sent for the literature immediately.

When it arrived, I showed it to Buddy, who muttered, "There you go again, with your damn initials. What's ME?"

"It stands for Marriage Encounter. It's for couples who want to enrich their marriages." He looked out the window.

"It's Catholic sponsored," I went on. I crossed myself and gazed upward. "Maybe people like Bing Crosby and Barry Fitzgerald will be there." He didn't laugh. "Anyway, it's non-sectarian. We can go."

Buddy glanced through the brochure. "It says, 'It's a

communication between a husband and wife through a weekend experience.' A weekend! What about my golf?"

Reading over his shoulder I countered, "We can 'get off the Modern World Treadmill, and take a fresh look at our marriage and priorities.' Please, Buddy, let's try it."

He lit a cigarette from the one he was smoking and inhaled deeply. "OK," came out a choking gasp.

We signed up for a fall weekend in Springfield, Illinois. Although I'm not religious, I prayed hard it would help. I could deny no longer that our marriage was in trouble.

Still I was optimistic. I went to Marriage Encounter with enthusiasm thinking, "This will save us." Buddy went with a cold.

A young boy with red hair and freckles took us to our assigned room, where we unpacked and left our watches in a drawer, as requested. No one was to care about time or schedules. I loved it.

Later (I couldn't tell when) we met with the others to learn about the program.

We were told there would be a series of talks by teams of trained married couples and a priest.

Rose and Jack were scheduled first, and they and Father John introduced themselves. Then the group did, too. Almost all the men seemed uncomfortable, fidgeting in their chairs. Most of the women (including me) were smiling nervously.

Rose cleared her throat and began. "The Marriage Encounter Weekend is a positive and personal experience for a couple. You'll receive techniques of loving communication here you can use the rest of your lives."

Father John, who looked nothing like Barry Fitzgerald, but seemed just as dear, said, "This is your opportunity to look deeply into your relationship with each other and with God. It's a time to share your feelings: fears, joys, frustrations - and hopes." I felt a holiness about it, a sweet mystique.

We learned what ME was not: a retreat, a marriage clinic or a sensitivity course.

Then we learned what it was: a positive, simple, common-sense experience between husband and wife that could revitalize marriage by helping couples see what their relationship can and should be.

We were encouraged to make a practice of writing ten-minute love letters to each other every day, romantic and tender. "Pretend you've just fallen in love. Really pour it on," Jack said, grinning.

Sex was never denied its importance, but we were reminded that too often it comes up too fast.

Communication skills were discussed, and we were advised not to be judgmental. "There is no right or wrong in a relationship," said Rose.

After a long question and answer period, Father John stretched and said, "May peace be with you," then added with a twinkle in his eye, "Now go to your rooms."

People laughed, but I had tears in my eyes. ME was perfect for us!

I saw our marriage as an angry, festering boil that needed to be lanced so the sticky stuff could ooze out. ME was the Red Cross, Clara Barton and Jesus Christ, who together, could cleanse, heal, and save us from damnation. How could we lose with a team like that?

As we walked down the corridor, I clutched Buddy's limp hand in mine and said, "We'll make it."

In our room I wasn't so sure.

I tried to use the communication techniques we'd just learned. "I like the idea that this is not a time to think of the past, but our future together, don't you?"

Buddy said, "Uh, yeah, that's nice," and sneaked a look at his watch in the drawer.

We wrote our love letters to each other. I was Elizabeth Barrett Browning. He was a math major completing his English assignment.

I tried to be romantic, tender - sexy. I didn't even care "if it came up too fast," but Buddy was afraid I'd catch his cold.

Somehow we made it through the weekend. It helped that we had kitchen privileges in the dormitory of the church and, thank God, that someone put wine in the fridge Saturday night. I didn't know it was the sacramental wine for Sunday mass, but Father John forgave me for drinking it. What else could a priest do?

We did try for several months to practice the techniques we'd learned at ME, but it seemed futile. I'd spend hours on my "ten minute" love letter. Often Buddy forgot to write his. And his cold persisted like a woman's headache.

In desperation I contacted several of the couples we'd met and we formed a pot-luck group to get together and reminisce about ME. It helped for a while, but only prolonged the inevitable.

Oddly enough, Buddy told me he loved the program and the people. He just thought it was too late for us. By that time I knew why.

The night Buddy and I decided to separate, Father John stopped by for a visit. I don't think he realized he was performing the last rites.

*****

Shortly after I moved to California, I saw a Marriage Encounter sticker on a car in the next lane on the freeway. I felt happy for the occupants, sad for me. I fumbled inside my purse for a hankerchief, preparing to weep as I passed by.

As I pulled alongside, I glanced over into their car expecting to see a radiant couple exuding happiness. Instead, I saw their faces, angry and surly. They looked ugly as they argued, so unhappy together.

I sped past them and didn't cry at all.

CHAPTER X

A SHORT WALK WITH
TONY ROBBINS

I began writing for "The La Jolla Report" while still keeping my executive job, "advertising manager."

Pat Dahlberg, the editor, noticed there was a "Firewalk Experience" seminar scheduled in San Diego at the round Holiday Inn. She asked me if I'd like to cover it.

After my reluctant, "OK," she said, "Great."

I remembered the discussion about it at GROW and how I had *not* put the experience on my TO DO list. Clearly, I had no burning desire to walk across hot coals.

Trying to feel more upbeat about my assignment, I thought at least I'll get to hear Anthony Robbins speak. Perhaps I could even meet him, now that I was a member of the press corps. (I did love to elevate my positions.)

*****

Tony Robbins entered the room exuding confidence. After greeting us warmly, he began his lecture.

"Walking unharmed over a bed of red hot coals can turn fear into power. You need this seminar of instruction to empower you to do it."

As we viewed a "Firewalk" video, I smelled smoke emanating from the coals outside.

"Think positive thoughts. Feel your strength. You can do it. 'Psychology Today' claims, "The experience is the most powerful vehicle for change in existence." I'd heard that at GROW.

He became more intense, more emotional – more fired up? "People are becoming mesmerized," I noted on my legal pad, a fascinated observer.

There were tips, too. "Don't look down," he warned. "One man did, and his feet blistered immediately."

I sensed he lost some of the crowd.

He won them back when he assured them all would be fine, if they kept their heads up and focused on his instructions. The seminar lasted several hours. When it ended, everyone followed him outside to the coals.

Those who were hyped-up most walked first. As they got to the other side (about fifteen feet across) I could see their exuberance. Lots of high fives and two thumbs up.

I had enough for my story and turned to leave, when I felt a massive hand on my head. "You're ready," Tony Robbins said from up high. (He was extremely tall.)

"Oh, no! I'm not. I'm just here to write about the seminar for a small newspaper. See my notes? I'm happy to meet you, though."

"You can do this. I know you can. Just keep your head up and follow me."

He trod the 1,200° coals solidly (but swiftly) to the other side.

I skittered across in hippity-hop fashion. But I made it! And with no sizzling. Just a tiny, tender spot on one little toe.

Had I been mesmerized, too? Perhaps, like watching someone else being hypnotized, I'd become transfixed myself. I'm not sure. I just knew that I felt the same exuberance of the others.

We spoke afterward to share our feelings. None of us understood the technical part: that our limited belief systems can be overcome with N.L.P., neurolinguistic programming.

Yet it must have been true. How else could we have walked over red hot coals without being burned?

Our consensus: it was a phenomenon, mystical and magical. Impossible to define.

But there was one fact we knew.

WE DID IT.

I still have the "Firewalk" t-shirt to prove it.

CHAPTER XI

est, ETC.

I rushed into my therapist's office wearing a red sweater, white slim pants and handsome silver jewelry I'd picked up in Old Town. I was looking better since I'd had my colors done. (I'm a winter.)

I noticed the clock on his desk showed ten minutes past the hour and, slithering into the leather chair, I apologized for being late. (He once told me I apologized too much. I responded, "I do? I'm sorry.")

"Lee. You wouldn't believe my schedule. And California is so big. I really find it hard to reach places on time. I set my watch ahead ten minutes, but it doesn't fool me anymore. I keep thinking I have an extra ten minutes."

I told him about the Firewalk Experience and how empowered I felt. "Lee, if I could do that, I can do anything."

Still on a high I continued, "Do you like my hair?" I swished it so he could see the cut. "I'm meeting someone new for lunch, and..."

He eased back in his swivel chair and said softly, "It hurts, doesn't it?"

Immediately, tears welled up in my eyes. I headed for the Kleenex, sank down on the couch and thought, God damn it, here we go again!

"Of course it hurts. When I arrived in California ten months ago, I felt as if I were in a leaky lifeboat heading out to sea. Even yesterday, while driving along in my car, I cried so hard I turned on the windshield wipers to see. (Sometimes I exaggerate.)

"But the low times are easing, both in depth and frequency. Everything I've been trying is helpful - and I don't like coming here to spend each session recapping the demise of my marriage. I'm sick of talking about it. I'm even getting bored yakking about Buddy and Barbara. It's enough. It's over. I want to go forward – learn from the past and build for the future." I stopped crying and dropped the wet Kleenex into my purse.

He said, "I want to build for your future, too, but not on a cracked foundation."

"Hey, Lee, most houses over fifty years old have cracked foundations. I want to undergo reconstruction, not build a bomb-shelter." I got up and moved back into the chair. "Besides, there's something new I want to talk about today. I've heard about est, and I want to sign up for the training."

He swiveled upright and asked, "Why?"

"Because, like the mountain, it's there. I want to try everything."

"What do you know about it?" he asked.

"Not much. I know in Latin it means 'it is,' and it's written with a small 'e' because it signifies nothing. I find that intriguing, I'm eager to discover what nothing's all about."

"I don't think you'll like it," Lee clasped his hands on the desk. "It's harsh and you're not ready for it. I strongly advise against it."

"But," I told him, "I need your permission. If I'm in therapy, I must have the approval of my therapist."

"I'm sorry, Francy. I can't give it to you."

I left the session angry. Why should he have such control over my life? The more I thought about it, the more determined I became to take the est training. (Persistence brings resistance; I was to find out soon.)

*****

While filling out my name tag at the est guest seminar, I literally felt my heart pounding. What was I getting myself into? Why was I there? I looked around nervously at three hundred others - looking around nervously at three hundred others. What did we hope to find?

est graduates steered us, bobbing white name tags, into one of the large halls on the concourse of the San Diego Civic Center. While waiting for the seminar to begin, I leafed through the literature I'd picked up from a table in the lobby.

I thought of ME as I discovered what est was not: group therapy, sensitivity training, encounter groups, positive thinking, meditation, psychology or therapy. In fact, the brochure said, "If you feel in need of therapy, psychological, psychiatric or medical services, you should see a psychologist, psychiatrist or physician."

After reading all that est wasn't, I tried to figure out what est could be. It seemed "nothing" was left. (So far, so good.) Then I found its statement of purpose: "To transform your ability to experience living so that the situations you have been trying to change, or have been putting up with for years, clear up, just in the process of life."

I read a quote from Werner Erhard, est's dynamic founder: "est is a sixty-hour experience which opens an additional dimension of living to your awareness."

It was confusing. In the statement of purpose, "experience" was used as a verb. In Werner's description, "experience" was a noun. Reading on, I discovered a better explanation. "Having someone tell you what it's like to parachute out of an airplane, is not the same as *experiencing* parachuting out of an airplane."

I thought about the zany script I'd concocted at the nudist colony, and its theme, "experiencing the experience is a wonderful experience." Could that be what the Latin "it is" is?

I began to feel the excitement in the room and turned, just in time to see the handsome leader of the seminar, Arnold, stride in to huge applause. The fervor rose as he swaggered around on the platform, attaching the microphone to his jacket. The est people on the sidelines helped create the hype.

Arnold, in his twenties, smooth and self-assured, began to shout out questions he well knew the answers to. "Do you want to continue sleepwalking or experience life?"

"Experience life!" came back a roar from the audience.

"Would you like true satisfaction or be assholes going through your acts, resisting the truth and blaming others for your life not working?"

"I don't want to be an asshole," I heard myself scream along with the others.

With the crowd's enthusiasm in full swing, Arnold began his pitch. "Through est you can 'get off it,' stop being pompous and defensive, step back and take a look at yourself. You can improve relationships, too. est's definition of love is giving people the space to be the way they are, and the way they are not."

He quoted Werner with reverence and regularity. "Werner says, 'Obviously the truth is what's so. Not so obvious is, it's also so what?' And, 'It's easier to ride a horse in the direction it's going.'" I wasn't so sure about "so what," but I liked the horse sense.

People in the audience were asked to share. After microphones were brought to them, they began unloading to the entire roomful of strangers pieces of their private, personal shit. Whether it was positive or negative stuff, the audience applauded, whistled, and yelled. It was similar to GROW, but on a different level. This was deep shit.

I looked around at those clamoring for the microphones to broadcast their drivel and felt repulsed. I started to leave, but something kept me there. Perhaps it was the honesty beneath the bullshit. Maybe I was just tired of being an asshole.

After the sharing period, we learned about the training. It's given during two week-ends (a Friday night, and all day Saturday and Sunday). Sessions would last until they were over, the trainers would decide when. Four in the morning was not unheard of.

We'd have straight chairs to sit on. Yes, we could bring pillows if we had bad backs. There would be rigid rules of silence, except when sharing, and few bathroom and meal breaks. Other rules: no alcohol, uppers or downers - only medicine prescribed by doctors and birth control pills. No smoking except on breaks. Arnold warned, "Be prepared for physical and emotional stress." Curiously, the more stringent the rules, the more intrigued I became.

When a gray-haired woman asked why the rules were so tough, Arnold answered mechanically, "Because they're the rules."

I found a quote from Werner that answered her question better: "In an attempt to avoid discomfort, uncertainty, pain, hunger ... just plain boredom, we smoke, make idle conversation and eat, when if we'd just be still, the meaninglessness of our lives, the pain we suppress would come to the surface and be experienced."

Arnold told us of est's insistence on keeping agreements. Truth, dependability and honor were stressed as integral. I liked that.

When the application forms were handed out, I took one and answered the questions quickly until I came to, "Are you in therapy at this time? If so, do you have your therapist's permission to take the training?" These were the questions I'd been dreading, and I deliberated before answering. Finally I checked "yes" to both.

I hated the deception, and felt not totally clean, like I'd taken a bath and put on dirty underwear. Yet, nothing could stop me now. On the lobby table, along with my name tag, I turned in my application for est.

✳✳✳✳✳

"OK, you assholes, get in your seats."

I should have been desensitized by the guest seminar; still, I was shocked. At the est training we were treated like a pack of animals, herded to the front of the room and the middle of each row, so that later arrivals could fill the back and outer seats. Actually, it made sense.

The est staff members on hand to assist were zombies. What was going on inside their heads? Their cool detachment seemed to indicate "nothing." Par for the course.

Our trainer, Robert, marched in woodenly after everyone was seated. Young and fair-haired, he looked like a member of a Hitler Youth gang. He began by accusing us of pretending our lives were working when they weren't. "Through est you can take charge. You can be the cause rather than the effect. No one needs to play victim anymore.

"Most of us go through life like machines," he continued. "We act and react, instead of feel. est lets us know we have choices. We can choose to experience life, and get in touch with feelings we've been avoiding for years. Or we can choose not to. 'I don't know' is also a choice - to evade responsibility. Inability to choose keeps us stuck in our lives."

I chose to get unstuck (without coming unglued), and take charge of my life.

I listened intently as Robert went on, "A word to remove from our vocabularies is 'try.' It doesn't make sense. It's impossible to try to move a desk. You either move it, or you don't."

He drew three circles on the blackboard and spoke about each. Inside the first one he wrote DO. "Most people think they'll be happy when they do something, like graduate from college or write a book." In the next circle he wrote HAVE. "Others think when they have a huge house or achieve success, they'll be happy then." Inside the last circle he wrote BE. He lowered his voice, "It makes the most sense just to be happy. Don't *try* to be happy, just *be* happy," he emphasized. "The past is history, and why live for the future? Real happiness is in the here and now."

"You can live your life 'on purpose' by going about it with intention, your eye on the goal." I thought of "on purpose" as "on target." Bullseye. The center to aim for.

Before asking the group to share (a part of every session) Robert told his "story": his life before est, then how est had transformed him.

"est is not about change, but transformation," he explained. "I used to be scared of everything. I even kept my seat belt buckled at a drive-in movie," he admitted with a smile. I laughed and people joined in. "Now I go parasailing and scuba diving; I experience life and I'm not afraid.

"My relationship with my parents has cleared up. We used to have no real communication, just angry dialogue. Now I know they're not the cause of my problems, and I don't lay that on them anymore. They like me better, too, and see me as a person, not just their son."

Underneath his austere exterior, Robert was human.

So far est was absorbing, but a lot to ingest and I began to feel drowsy. It's funny, I used to go on fourteen-hour plane trips to Europe and never fall asleep. But during the est training, on my metal folding chair surrounded by swarms of people, I dozed a lot. We were told it was OK. We could sleep through the training and still get it.

I woke up from a snooze when Robert began to talk about the processes we'd be going through. He said, "You'll meet yourself from three standpoints: the social person, the person hiding under a mask and who you really are. You are going to be intimidated, insulted, frightened, humiliated, nauseated and enraged. You might vomit, cry, shake, have bellyaches and headaches. But the processes are a central, necessary part of the training, so get ready for the first one.

"Close your eyes. Thank you. Get comfortable. Let your hands be loose on your lap. Good. Notice your body, how you feel. Thank you."

We were led through many parts of our bodies, even our hearts and livers, to bring them into our consciousness and feel them. I felt my heart pulsating. I wasn't sure where my liver was, but I became aware of a lump inside me, and hoped that was it.

He continued, "Notice sounds around you, and smells. Expand your space. Bring your chair in with you. Bring in the people on either side of you. Thank you. Recall the room. Recall a time when you were happy. Remember how you moved, acted and felt. Good."

The processes often began like that, guided imagery of a sort. Then we were led deeper and deeper into our subconscious, always given instructions, often to remember sad and painful times as well as safe and happy moments. Sometimes I heard laughter and chuckles; other times I heard sobbing, screaming and wailing. Was it mass hypnosis, mass hysteria - or both?

The truth process was the most powerful experience for me. We were asked to pick something that was bothering us, a problem, a feeling, a situation we weren't handling. We stretched out on the floor for this one. Again we closed our eyes and were led into ourselves. "Feel your right foot. Thank you. Now feel the bones in it. Good."

Drifting deep into my unconscious, I suddenly began to relive vividly the most shameful experience of my life. I was in a sleazy, dark motel room and I was - Oh God - I was with another man. (I hadn't "been" with anyone except Buddy in my whole life.)

In the glowing green light from the neon sign flashing through the window, I saw the sex clearly, and wanted to vomit. Pain, an erupting geyser, began in my vagina and spread through my entire body.

"BUDDY, why did you leave me so much?"

*****

Beside necessary business, there was golf.

On our honeymoon in Banff, the Sunday after we were married, I awoke at 8:30 to see a note on his pillow.

"Good morning, honey. I'm golfing. Be back soon."

I dimly remembered he golfed. In our five-year courtship, he never chose to, if he could be with me.

He didn't return until 2:30.

"Sorry darling," he said. (Now I was "darling"!) "I only intended to play nine holes, but I hooked up with a Scotsman and we ended up on the other side of the mountain and, well, we thought we'd play the back nine in," he said all in one breath.

It sounded logical, but I still felt hurt.

And hungry! Thinking he'd be back soon, I waited to have breakfast with him. I never thought to order breakfast (or lunch) for myself. Disgruntled, at the very least, I thought, "What a lousy way to start a marriage."

It didn't get better. Golf became a Sunday ritual after "the honeymoon was over."

Before the children were born, I was lonely without him – the golf widow everyone jokes about.

After the children arrived, I wasn't lonely. But, especially after the fourth baby was delivered fourteen months after the third, I could have used his help.

I also regretted we couldn't enjoy a family day together.

Sadly, the ritual continued. He'd leave home at 8:00, return at 2:30, have lunch, take a nap and at 5:00 would ask, "What does everybody want to do today?"

Exacerbating my aggravation was the fact that he played several times a week, too.

I once asked him, "You'd sell your soul for golf, wouldn't you?"

"Yes," was his instant retort.

This was becoming a real problem in our marriage. I suggested seeing Dan Kiley about it.

I was sure we could work out something fair, like nine holes every week, or eighteen every other.

But Buddy replied, "I can't do that. I'm in a foursome that plays eighteen holes every Sunday. If you want me to stop playing...."

"No," I said with my head lowered. "I know how much you love it."

"Thanks," he said with obvious relief.

I should have called his bluff.

After winning his gamble, he upped the ante.

Brazenly, he added volleyball, then tennis too. I folded when he began to jog. He certainly had his balls.

Did I want to get even?

You bet!

I had run the gamut from disgruntled to rage. Realizing this, I made a last-ditch effort to control it (an appointment with Dan Kiley).

I asked him, "Did Buddy not want to be with me because i nagged, or did I nag because he didn't want to be with me?"

"That's a 'who came first, the chicken or the egg' question - impossible to answer."

I decided to analyze the problem myself.

Buddy was the villain (hiss). I was the victim (poor me) who'd "gotten even" by committing a foul deed (alas).

To be fair, the melodrama I staged was not totally honest.

Actually, Buddy was a nice guy who loved sports.

I was his wife who wanted more of him than he could give.

My foul deed, alas, remained dastardly.

In the truth process, my struggle to justify getting even, with the "poor me" scenario, didn't ring true.

*****

Still deep in my unconscious, now instead of whining, I sobbed loudly, "Buddy, I'm so sorry."

My shoulders ached with guilt I'd carried for years.

The erupting geyser, internal before, now became an out-of-body experience. It oozed out like the yellow mass forced from an old wen of mine. I'd been embarrassed by the stench.

We had been told, "Notice sounds around you, and smells."

Incredulously, I smelled that exact, vile odor again.

Amazed, I sat up Buddha-like and remembered Werner's statement, "Obviously, the truth is what's so. Not so obvious is, it's also so what."

I heard myself scream, "SO WHAT?"

I wasn't being crass or flippant. I just got that it was history - and there was nothing I could do to change the past. Nothing.

Miraculously the noxious odor dissipated. And so did the pain.

I thought of something Robert, our trainer, had said earlier. "There are no accidents in the universe. You are exactly where you are meant to be."

After Rebirthing, I'd acknowledged my separation from Buddy as destined, but I had equated destiny with fate. Now I realized *I* was responsible for the turn in my life. I had chartered my own course and since "there are no accidents in the universe," I was where I belonged.

I came out of the truth process weak, but strong - if that makes sense.

It doesn't, but it doesn't have to.

*****

est went on - and on. Different things came up for me in other processes, but nothing ever so intense again.

Late in the day of the second weekend, I was sleeping peacefully on my uncomfortable chair when I awoke to delirious cheering in the room.

Alan (we had different trainers for every session) was pointing to the mathematical astronomical equations on the blackboard, and shouting in a hoarse voice, "If you didn't get it, stand up." I rose with about half the people there.

He repeated the information on the blackboard, calculating again the enormity of our universe and space.

The meaning of est we were to get was our cosmic insignificance. We're miniscule. We're not even fly specks. In proportion to the world of space, we are less than microscopic. We are nothing; our lives are nothing. Knowing that, how can our difficulties be of any possible significance or consequence?

By that time, most of the people were vigorously nodding in agreement and laughing gleefully, ecstatic in the release of what had seemed insurmountable problems in their lives.

Alan went up to each person who remained standing to ask again, "Did you get it?" He convinced almost all of them that they did, and they sat down.

When he asked me if I got it, I said, "About forty-percent."

"What about the other sixty-percent?"

"Bullshit."

He said, "Good, you got it."

Weary, I succumbed and sat down. What I wanted most in life at that moment was to go home, take a hot bath and go to sleep in a bed.

One man refused to sit down, insisting he didn't get it. He was told it was too late to get his money back (three hundred-fifty dollars), but he said, "I don't care," and walked out to cheers. Many supported him for telling the truth as he saw it.

The next week, I pulled out the est literature from under my bed and read over more quotes from Werner: "est is a uniquely personal experience. After taking the training, you probably won't know *how* it works; you will only know *that* it works.

"It's like reading a book on bicycle riding. You know about balancing on a bicycle in one way. If you sit on a bicycle and fall off a couple of times, you now know the same thing, but in a new way. At that moment when it clicks and you can balance on the bike and actually ride it, you have not learned anything new. You just know what you knew before, but you know it in an entirely different way."

I shoved the est literature back under my bed and sat very still on the floor for a long time.

It was a puzzle: If I hadn't learned anything new, what was it I knew before that I knew in a new way now? Nothing. The goddamn answer was nothing! Everything's the same, only shifted, transformed. The universe is still all around me. I'm just not at the center of it anymore.

My new license plates say, "O I GOT IT."

(Werner Erhard's say, "SO WUT.")

CHAPTER XII

THE HEDGES CAPERS

After est, therapy was everything I needed in life - and less. Every time I'd soar upward on a new high, I'd plummet down to Earth in Lee's office. I told him about est, of course. After the fact. What a session!

"You lied about my permission?" he asked, grasping the arms of his chair in a death grip. His professional cloak was beginning to fray.

"Yes, and I hated I had to. I understand your reluctance to let me go. You were trying to protect me. But, Lee, I'm tougher than you think. It's true, est *is* harsh, yet it was good for me."

"How? Tell me about it." Color returned to his knuckles; still he continued to sit erect in his chair.

"Well, I didn't buy the whole package. I never would accept that my life is nothing. We've worked too hard to repair my fractured ego, right?"

He didn't respond.

"However, 'I got that' (I purposely used 'est-hole' jargon) my problems are not the most important things in life. I'd become so obsessed with my pain, I was a pain in the ass. No wonder Marcy and Rick bought me a camera - to focus outward."

"You've been introspective, of course. You need time to grieve, to mourn your loss. If you don't get your pain out now, it will be worse for you later." Was he trying to justify his sixty dollars an hour?

"Est jolted out a lot of pain!" I told him about the truth process and he listened quietly. "I moved through a light year of heavy-duty stuff. I not only accept my life now, I'm ready to live it. I want to quit therapy."

He leaned forward in his chair and asked, "How can you stop now, just when you're getting close to something?"

I strung along for more sessions, all downward cycling. Finally, unhappy with my progress (in the wrong direction) I decided to get a second opinion.

When my friend, Ruth, suggested I see Hedges Capers, I asked, "Is that his real name?" She nodded, and I laughed. "It sounds like the title of a British spy story, THE HEDGES CAPERS." I pronounced the name in a clipped, English accent.

Smiling, she replied, "He has a title, but it's 'Founder and Director of the San Diego Institute of Transactional Analysis.' He's a good therapist, too."

"Great. I need one."

****

"Call me Hedge, everybody does. Find a comfortable spot to sit, anywhere you like." I chose an easy chair, kicked off my shoes and tucked my feet up under me. It felt cozy in the den of Hedges Capers' La Jolla Boulevard home.

Looking over at him, sprawled in the huge chair opposite me, I liked what I saw. He had beautiful gray, almost white hair. His slim, lanky frame was dressed casually in a pale yellow t-shirt and khaki pants. The beach sandals seemed logical with the ocean so close.

79

Stretching his feet out on the ottoman, he settled back in his chair and said, "Tell me about yourself."

I began with an overview of my life in California, then flashed back to the story between the bookends (shoved together in a condensed version). I sped through it, striving hard to make it to the finish without crying, but lost the race. "Damn!" I sputtered. "I wanted to prove to you I'm OK. Guess I blew it, didn't I?"

Hedge asked, "Do you have a belly-button?"

I nodded, a bit taken aback.

"Well, then - that makes you human just like everybody else, doesn't it?" He reached for an orange from the fruit bowl near him and tossed it to me. "Welcome to California, Francy. I'm glad you're here. You did a good thing by moving and starting over. Besides being gutsy, you're bright."

My cheeks became wet again, and he asked, "Why are you crying now?"

"These are happy tears," I explained. "I'm delighted with my progress report and - touched that you think me bright."

"Don't you think you are?"

"No. Not really. I never have. Even when I became a life master at bridge, I attributed it to my card sense. My brother's the smart one in the family. My sister's the achiever. She…"

"What about you?"

"I play Gracie Allen a lot. You know, act dumb to make people laugh." I gazed down at the orange in my lap.

He said, "Don't kid yourself. Gracie Allen was a very smart woman."

I thought a moment, then looked up. "She was, wasn't she?" I peeled my orange and Hedge and I shared it.

We discussed TA and I told him how it had helped our family.

"I'm glad," he said. "TA's a good tool."

"Yes, it showed us how to communicate."

"Don't use big words, just say 'talk.' The simpler the better. Words can lose their power if they're overworked."

"I know what you mean. 'Special' and 'unique' aren't special and unique anymore, are they?"

He smiled.

We delved into the past again, my problems and my guilt.

He told me, "If you want a judge, go to a clergyman - or a mother. Criticism is negative. Friends don't criticize each other, if they're really friends. Being caring and constructive, that's what counts."

"As a therapist, and my new friend, what can you tell me that's caring and constructive?" I asked.

"I think you're a lovely woman who's suffered enough. Everyone's problems are magnified under a microscope, and who doesn't have some turkey stuff?" Removing his feet from the ottoman, he said, "Why don't you go out and live your life? If problems arise, come back and we'll talk some more."

"Talk, not communicate, right?"

"Right. You're a fast learner. As I said before, you're bright."

"Certainly. I'm Shirley McLaine!"

Rising from our comfortable chairs, I said, "Oh, I almost forgot. My therapist thinks I'm getting close to something."

"You are."

"Close to what?"

"Quitting!" We laughed together and he walked me to the door.

As we hugged good-bye, he said, "You mentioned bridge. We'll have to get together sometime for a game with Tom and Amy."

"Tom and Amy who?"

"Harris. Perhaps you've heard of Tom. He wrote *I'm OK, You're OK*."

****

Several months later, Hedge called to tell me about a five-day workshop the Institute was planning.

"I think it would be good for you, Francy. It's powerful. Some people come back to it every year, even from Europe."

"Hedge, I'm not sure I'll be in town. I'm going home - I mean to Illinois - on the tenth, and..."

"The workshop is from the fifth to the ninth."

"Oh. That's cutting it close. I have lots to do before I leave – shop for clothes, get a perm, take a make-up lesson. I'm going back to file for divorce and sell my house, and I want to look great for the festivities!"

"Spruce up on the inside, too, and you'll be really beautiful."

"Go for it all, right?" I laughed. "Why not? OK. Count me in. I can use all the fortification I can get."

Hedge welcomed me to the workshop with a hug. After introducing me to the people there, he said, "Help yourself to coffee and croissants ... there's fruit, too." Then he ambled off to greet the next arrival. The atmosphere, gracious and creature-comfortable, certainly was a contrast to est.

There were twenty-two of us. As everyone mingled and chatted, I felt a bubbling excitement. Those who'd met at previous workshops were thrilled to see each other again. Most of us attending for the first time were apprehensive, yet eager to begin. As we got seated, I looked over the interesting mix of men and women from such places as San Diego, Phoenix, Indianapolis and Stockholm, and wondered what common denominator had brought us together.

Hedge began the workshop by introducing the co-leader, his son, Hedges, Jr. A boyish thirtyish, he didn't look like his dad, but had the same warmth and a similar smile. He was a therapist, too.

The first thing he told us was, "You don't need to call me Hedge Junior. Hedge or Hedges will do."

Roland, who was from Stockholm, asked, "How will you know when we mean your dad?"

"Good question. That's why we like to get this name business settled up front. When Dad and I work together, usually one of us goes by 'Hedge,' the other 'Hedges.'"

"Which one is which?" asked Roland.

"We switch around." He joined us in our laughter and said, "I'll be Hedges, OK, Dad?"

Together, "the Hedges" gave us basic information. Most of the sessions would be held where we were sitting, a separate structure on the grounds of the Capers' home. Sometimes we'd meet outside on the lawn. I liked the informality, but, anxious after the first ten minutes, five days seemed interminable.

Hedge said, "You're all invited to dinner the evenings we meet. Weekend lunches will be out on your own."

Susan, the woman next to me, leaned over and whispered, "Lunch tomorrow?"

I nodded, "Yes." She looked like someone I'd like to know.

Hedge began telling us about the workshop. "Some of what we do here can be found in books. Some things I make up," he admitted with a smile. "Whatever works for people, I salt away and use again. Here's a good exercise I like to start with. Get relaxed, then inhale slowly, as deeply as you can. Hold while I count to ten. Now expel air, even more slowly, through barely open lips." He waited while we exhaled, then said, "Repeat."

As we continued the exercise, the pressure at the back of my neck eased, and I began to feel light. When the group shared individual reactions, we discovered many experienced the same buoyancy. Probably it was all that air.

Hedges told us, "You can do this exercise any time you feel stress. Why don't you try it when you're stopped at a traffic light and in a hurry? It won't make the red light change faster, but you won't care as much."

To a smiling group of people Hedge threw out, "Let's break and go up to the house."

Dinner was an informal buffet, a nutritious combination of cold health foods and steaming hot Mexican dishes. Hedge's wife (a hugger, too) was a handsome woman, her cropped, white hair stunning against her tan. Wearing a comfortable outfit and low, leather shoes, she was a serene hostess with everything under control.

And Hedge loved playing host, mixing his guests like a well-tossed salad. Happy for the opportunity to become better acquainted, we liked it when he came around to "stir us up" and rearrange us.

I felt at home. I looked forward to the next four days (were there only four left?) and sensed our friendly group would seem like family before the workshop ended.

Saturday's session began with Hedge telling us how important it was to create, in our minds, a safe place for the child within us. Then, in times of stress or pain, we'd have it available – our special spot where we could retreat and find peace. It seemed a lovely idea to have a protected haven, a port in a storm.

"Pick a partner," he instructed, "to figure out together where your safe place might be."

My partner, Marilyn, knew hers immediately. It was at her family's kitchen table where she'd kneaded bread through the years. With her eyes closed, she said smiling, "I hear my children playing around me. I can even smell the yeast. This place is right for me." She opened her eyes and we talked about it. Then she said, "OK, Francy, it's your turn."

The first spot I thought of was my sunshiny den in Illinois, but that was out. When Marilyn suggested I try somewhere in my California condominium, I told her, "I can't, I'm moving next month." Anticipating her next question, I added, "My new condo won't work either. It's empty, with only concrete floors." I felt in limbo, lost. Even Marilyn couldn't help me.

Disillusioned, I called Hedge over. "I'm stumped," I told him, "I can't find a safe place for myself anywhere."

He said gently, "It doesn't have to be real. Imagine someplace wonderful, where no harm can come to you, ever."

I closed my eyes and remembered the painting that hung over my fireplace in Illinois. The blue lake in the foreground looked isolated, yet tranquil. I sat down at the edge of the water and grew quiet. A moment later, I squeezed Hedge's hand and said, "Thanks."

When it was time to break for lunch, I looked for Susan. Before I could spot her, Hedges announced, "Have lunch today with the person you relate to the least."

I knew who that person was. Helen, perhaps ten years my senior, had a face disfigured on one side. It was difficult to look at her, yet difficult not to. I felt uneasy around her. Must we have lunch together? I didn't want to. What about Susan? Just then I saw Helen - walking towards *me!*

"Shall we have lunch?" she asked. Her lopsided smile was the best she could muster.

"Yes, let's do." I wondered how I could. Would I be able to swallow my food? She wasn't appetizing to look at anywhere, but across a lunch table...?

As we got into her '65 Ford, I asked, "Where shall we go?"

"How about Su Casa? They have good margaritas."

"Margaritas sound great!" I said, and meant it.

We ordered chile rellenos and the medium-size margaritas. (The giant size was colossal.)

We made small talk about the workshop; this was her third one with Hedge, and so far she liked it best. Then the subject shifted to our broken marriages. I was surprised to learn she'd initiated her divorce. I couldn't imagine anyone - with a face like that - wanting out of a marriage.

She told me, "The man I was married to was awful. I didn't love him, and couldn't live with him any longer." I admired her spunk and asked more about her life.

"I'm getting my degree in counseling; in fact, Hedge's workshops count toward my hours. I live in a small community in Northern California, where there are no therapists. Since my cancer and surgery on my face, I've had lots of counseling. Now I want to help others and give back."

"Helen, that's wonderful. I'm proud of you." I took a long sip of my margarita, then added, "I'm sorry about your cancer. I didn't know what happened to your cheek, and was embarrassed to ask. Are you all right now?"

"Yes. I used to be pretty, and that made it harder. But I'm fine now, inside and out. I accept reality and deal with the truth. Even at my ex-husband's funeral..."

"Oh, I didn't know he died."

"Yes, last year. When I went to his funeral, I leaned over his coffin and spoke to him."

She paused, and I fantasized her words, "Oh my darling, I still love you. I'm sorry you're dead." (Is that what *I* would have said, had it been Buddy?) "Helen, tell me, what did you say?"

"Well, I looked down at him and under my breath, said, 'People are watching me now, so I have to act respectful, but - if you think I'm going to miss you, you son of a bitch - you're crazy!'"

I almost spilled my drink. Then I laughed so hard, people around us stared. Laughing with me, we threw money on the table, and the two of us, giggling like school girls, ducked out of the restaurant together. When we finally stopped, I looked right at her. "Helen, you're beautiful," I said. And meant it.

The session after lunch was held on the lawn. "Write down everything you're afraid of," Hedges told us. Remembering the lists I'd made at GROW, I headed this one FEAR.

In hodge-podge, disjointed, barely legible form, I jotted down in a small notebook all the fears I could think of.

1. I'm afraid of not making it.
2. I'm afraid I'll feel pain on my trip to Illinois.
3. I'm afraid of playing Gracie Allen.

There were seven variations on the same theme.

When we all finished writing, we were asked to tell our fears and discuss them. Opening up was difficult, and nobody was forced to. But, one by one, we began divulging secret fears we'd never before confided to anyone. Some were deep-seated; some were anxieties.

Mary, pretty, but overweight, told us, "I've always been afraid to compete with other women. I keep getting fatter, so I don't have to."

Arthur said, "I have a real fear of cancer. My whole family died of it. Why in hell do I smoke?"

With her head bent, Edythe admitted she was scared of being too sexual. "I love to try new positions, and my husband is a missionary (at least, in bed)."

As we talked about our fears, we were amazed (and relieved) to discover how many were similar. Disclosing our dark secrets, we felt lighter and, in the intimacy of sharing, bonded together. It was a good exercise. We learned the advantages of getting an intangible, like fear, into a written form so we could see it, face it and handle it better.

"Even pain can be pictured," Hedge told us. "When you experience it, visualize it. Give your pain size, shape - even color. If it has dimension, you can practice making it shrink and disappear." He led us through guided imagery, similar to est, to show us how.

During the discussion afterward, I shared, "My pain was a jagged, black boulder. I managed to reduce it to a gray stone, but it still felt rough around the edges."

"You got it down in size and lightened it. That's good. You'll smooth it out eventually. Keep practicing," said Hedge. "Someday, what you learn here will all soak in."

"Then life will be easier," added Hedges. "Here's a great exercise involving positive thinking and common sense. Use it often; make it automatic. Whenever you're in a painful, fearful or even aggravating situation, take a deep breath and ask yourself, "What's the worst thing that can happen?" Even if the answer is death, your acknowledging that is the first step toward dealing with it. But usually, situations aren't that dire, and the worst thing that can happen is you may miss a plane. It's an inconvenience, but not worth a heart attack. You can catch the next one."

That night I slept fitfully. In my dreams I missed my flight to the Midwest and the appointment with my lawyer. I saw the movers shatter my precious Steuben goblets, wedding gifts now worth many times their original value. I felt pain.

Thank God, I'd learned what to do. I jumped into my blue lake and swam to shore where I was safe. Exhaling slowly through barely open lips, I pictured my stomach ache a giant pumpkin, then shrunk it to a kumquat. I caught the next plane, rescheduled my lawyer's appointment, took a deep breath and asked myself what's the worst that can happen if my good glasses get broken? I was at the dime store buying plastic water tumblers when I woke up.

The workshop had soaked in. Not only was I saturated - I was inundated!

The last night at dinner, Hedge and I took our plates into the den. Our group didn't need mixing anymore. Just as I'd predicted, we'd become a family – Helen and I were the closest. Hearing the voices of the others in the next room, I wondered aloud, "What brought us all here, Hedge?"

"Oh, your pressure cookers probably needed simmering down. It's good to let off steam now and then, and this is a good place to learn how to do it. Mostly, I see you as people who just wanted to take some time for yourselves."

"Thanks for getting me here. I'll handle Illinois a lot better. Actually, the hardest part will be giving up my house. This year I've been in California, I've known it was there, intact, waiting for my return. How can I tell my home a final good-bye without crying?"

"How long did you live in it?"

"Over twenty years."

"You raised your children there?"

"Yes. When we moved in, our eldest was eight, our baby five months."

"You must have wonderful memories."

"Oh, I do."

"Then you'll always have them, won't you?"

We discussed adjusting to losses in life, and he told me about his friend and mentor, Eric Berne (who wrote *Games People Play*). "He had a marvelous mind. He was a genius who knew how to write. He certainly was a good friend of mine. I loved that man. Francy, I was so angry that he died, can you believe it took me a year to forgive him?"

I nodded slowly, then asked, "Hedge, do you have a belly-button?"

He threw his head back and laughed hard. Then we joined the others, arm in arm.

At the end of the evening, the group began difficult good-byes. Embraces, even between the men, showed real affection, and we all vowed to keep in touch. "I'm not a good correspondent," I said, "but I'll call everyone."

"Me, too?" asked Roland.

"Sure. On *my* phone bill, Stockholm won't make a dent."

Helen and I walked out together and she confided to me, "I didn't want to invite you to lunch that day."

"I'm glad you did," I said.

"So am I." She climbed into her rattletrap car, blew a kiss to me and drove off.

When I got home, I eyed my suitcase open on the couch and swallowed hard. I pulled out my notebook and scanned the fears I'd scrawled out. Then on a fresh page, in meticulous handwriting, I began a new list: *CONFIDENCE.*

1. I am confident I'll make it, because I already have.

2. I am confident I'll feel pain on my Illinois trip, but I'll handle it.

3. I am confident Gracie Allen was laughed at for acting dumb, but recognized for her brightness and the fun she added to life.

As I paralleled each fear, my confidence zoomed. By the time I completed the whole list, I felt phenomenal. I had the power of Atlas and Mohammed Ali's punch. Ready to take on the world, Illinois would be a cinch.

I filled my suitcase in ten minutes. The workshop notebook was the first thing I packed.

CHAPTER XIII

DEFOGGING IN ILLINOIS

My house looked different. Maybe it was the dead plants. I winced, but glanced past them. A visitor in my own home, I felt remote. I was different, too.

When I saw Pam and Peggy, we sat on the floor in the den and held hands like young children, jabbering fast to catch up on the past year. Being together again felt special. I'd missed my Illinois kids tremendously.

The doorbell chimed, ringing in the first of what became an entourage of people stopping by to say hello, view "the body" and pay their last respects. It was a wake.

I consoled children, friends, relatives and neighbors. Then I announced, "Hey, I'm Alive and Well and Living in La Jolla! I even have the stationary to prove it." A few people laughed politely.

With my chin thrust out, I added, "I really am OK. I discovered I'm a survivor. Distance helps." I ordered in pizza and beer, and "the wake" went on until one o'clock in the morning.

My divorced friend, Sheila, was the last one to leave. The crickets were chirping in the soft darkness, as I walked her to her car. "I wish I could move away," she said wistfully.

"If you want to, you can," I replied.

The next morning, I met with my lawyer. I had chosen him wisely. Tall, with dark, deep-set eyes and shaggy, black hair, he was a young Abe Lincoln.

"You look a lot better than the last time I saw you," he commented. "What have you done to yourself?"

"Nothing much." The new purple suit fit well, my subtle eye make-up looked deceptively unstudied, the fresh perm was a good one and my workshop notebook (with the confidence page dog-eared) was secure in my purse. "Just everything." We both smiled.

"How are the proceedings proceeding?" I asked.

He rustled some papers on his desk and said, "Not forward. Buddy's lawyer isn't sure yet about the settlement. He's trying to straighten out assets and liabilities."

"I'll talk to Buddy and see what I can untangle."

I called him that afternoon. "Hi, I'm in town and I'd like to see you about the divorce settlement," I said, all in one breath.

"Hi, Francy. The kids told me you were here. Are you OK?"

"Yes. You?"

"Uh huh. We can discuss the settlement, but I don't think it's a good idea for us to see each other."

"Right. What's the best time for you?"

"Maybe you didn't understand. We can work it out on the phone, but..."

"I understand. Is nine better than ten tomorrow morning?"

He laughed and asked, "Hey, did you take an assertive training course, or what?"

"Or what. Nine works for me."

We met at nine o'clock the next morning in pouring-down rain, in the last row of a public golf course parking lot. He didn't want Barbara to know he was seeing me.

I got into his car and looked at him. He was grayer, but still handsome. Damn! But his white patent-leather shoes were tacky. I felt better.

I became amused at the two of us hiding in the steamy car with the billows of smoke from his cigarettes adding to the fog around us. It was ludicrous. Yet, with the wipers flapping back and forth across the windshield, and the defogger exerting its valiant, best effort to clear the air, Buddy and I decided a realistic market

91

price for our house, and worked out a fair and amicable divorce settlement. I called my lawyer and told him.

Odd, the hushed "D" word, finally spoken, "divorce," was explicit - and far less ominous than the whisper.

*****

The movers came early the next day and, in answer to my persistent questions, assured me, "Of course we know how to pack glasses." I watched to make sure.

After looking in on Pam and Peg's rummage sale on the porch (and buying my own pot holders back from them) I went upstairs to box the remainder of my worldly possessions. I stopped only to go out for dinner with my mother-in-law, who needed to be absolved from the guilt she was feeling.

Pam was packing, too. She'd decided to move to California and live with me, temporarily, until she could find her own place. We were going to be a team. I'd help her drive her car west; she'd help me move into my larger condominium.

Peggy would remain at the University of Illinois to attend summer school and get her master's degree in journalism.

Telling Peg good-bye was heartbreaking. Even after Pam and I took off down the street, Pam backed up the car, and we both jumped out to hold her one more time. She clung to us too, but like a soft ragdoll, went limp when we let her go.

Tearfully returning to the car, I said, "Let me drive first, Pam. I want to."

She cleared her throat nervously and said, "Mom, you do remember my car's a stick shift, don't you"

"A what?!" I hadn't driven a stick shift since high school.

Pam talked me through it, and I got the car moving into first. When it gasped for second, I was waving to Peg and forgot the clutch. The first few blocks were bumpy but we were on our way.

There barely had been time to get melodramatic about bidding my house a final farewell, although I had allowed myself the luxury of a few tears the night before. Our family had had wonderful years there, but they were over. I'd always have memories.

I shifted into fifth and winked at Pam. Illinois had been a cinch. Except for the itchy rash creeping up my neck, I felt phenomenal.

CHAPTER XIV

SPEEDING TO CALIFORNIA

From the outset, Pam and I took the high road. On our trek west from Illinois, we predicted our time together would be jolly fun – a rare experience to treasure forever.

We traveled through three states planning beach picnics, trips to the zoo and jaunts to Mexico. We hugged often.

The first night of the trip, before flopping into bed in our turquoise motel room in Eureka, Kansas, we affirmed our alliance with a staunch handshake: partners, roommates, a mother-daughter team.

By the third day, our fervor had faded.

The fun junket had become a tiresome trip. Imprisoned in my captive seat belt, I just wanted it to be over.

As we neared the California border, I thought of Nelly, my horse at camp, who'd gallop wild-eyed and at full speed back to the stable. Aching to reach home, I was wild-eyed, too.

I shook my fist at a plane soaring overhead. "Jesus," I muttered, "it's going to break the goddamn sound barrier!" Weary of crawling on land, inching our way across the map, I longed to be on that plane. I yearned for a headset, at least, with a choice of music channels. The constant rock and roll blaring from Pam's radio was drumming its beat on my eyeballs.

"Did you say something, Mom?" Pam shouted over the din.

"Can't you drive faster? That plane must have landed in Hawaii by now." I was angry at the entire passenger list.

"Keep cool. We'll get there eventually."

"Next month - at this speed."

She told me, "Mom, I'm riding on two speeding tickets now. If I get another one, I could lose my license."

"I know." She'd told me before.

"But look at this desolate stretch. We haven't seen another car for miles. Who'll spot us? Can't you go a little faster - please?"

"You're wheedling," she said, mimicking me to perfection. (I said that a lot during child-rearing years.) Still, she readjusted her rear-view mirror, shrugged one shoulder and accelerated.

Speeding along on that desolate stretch we heard the police siren. Its shrillness pierced even the hard rock blaring from the radio. Pam shouted obscenities into the desert air and, with the highway patrol on her Honda hatch-back, she braked to a stop. "Pam, I feel terrible. It's my fault. That cop must have been hiding behind a cactus. What a louse. I hate people who play games, don't you?" She didn't answer.

Like an idiot I whispered, "Let's trade seats, and I'll get the ticket."

She glared at me and said, "I'll handle this. Promise you'll stay in the car."

She got out and resolutely walked back to meet the patrolman striding toward her.

I twisted in my seat, then swung over on my knees to peer out through the rear window. The red and blue flashing lights looked menacing even in the daylight.

Why had I promised to stay in the car? *I* was the mother. What were they saying? It looked like a silent movie. Poor Pam. Where was the popcorn?

Suddenly - I couldn't believe it - she and the patrolman were smiling and shaking hands.

Minutes later, she was back in the car waving him a chipper good-bye as he drove off with a salute.

I saluted back, then asked, "Pam, for God sakes, what happened?"

She grinned and cupped her hands together above her head like a boxer who'd just won a knock-out bout.

"Mom, I knew I had to fight for my life, but I couldn't think up a respectable lie outrageous enough for him to believe."

"So what did you tell him?"

"I told him the truth. I guess that's outrageous enough."

"What do you mean? C'mon Pam, what did you say?"

I told him, "Officer, my mom's getting a divorce in Illinois, and she can't wait to get to California where we're moving. I've been trying to keep within the speed limit, but she's really been pressing me. I have two tickets back east because I'm so stressed out about my parents' divorce, and I'd appreciate it if you could just give me a warning this time."

"What did he...?"

"He said, 'I've heard a lot of stories in my day, but nobody's ever come up with one like that. OK, you've got your warning, if you promise not to exceed the speed limit no matter what your mother says!'"

"Did you promise?"

"Of course! Then he said, 'Wish your mom good luck for me, I'm getting divorced myself and I know it's tough. You take it easy now, too, OK? Everything will work out.'"

Pam and I congratulated each other on the luck of the draw - *not* getting a happily married cop.

I drove the rest of the way at fifty-five miles per hour listening to symphonies. I'd pushed through a new rule: the driver got her choice of music.

When Pam saw the California welcome sign at the border, she squealed, "Mom, stop!" Exuberant, she climbed to the top of her car and did her boxer routine again.

I snapped her picture with the sign in the background. It was the first photo she entered into her new scrapbook, "California"!

CHAPTER XV

VACUUMING SUCKS

When we arrived at my condominium in La Jolla, Pam surveyed the disarray in silence. Boxes were stacked high, and items to be packed heaped in piles all over. My semi-precious junk had accumulated in a year.

Her first words were, "How do we start?"

I crooked my index finger and motioned, "follow me." We began the best way possible - with a walk on the beach.

Strolling barefoot along the ocean in the warm dusk, we kicked up sand and talked about how lucky we were. Suddenly she jumped three feet high in the air and whooped, "We made it, didn't we?"

She jogged ahead, then, frolicking like a puppy, circled back to me.

"The air is fresh out here. I can breathe better," she announced.

I slipped my arm around her waist and said, "So can I."

Moving into the new condominium was hard. At every crisis I asked myself, "What's the worst thing that can happen?" I kept finding out.

No one told me that before moving companies can unload one lamp, they must have a check for the entire bill. With the Illinois movers immobile in my driveway, I pounded on the door of my bank at 8AM - which didn't open officially until 10.

Thanks to the kindness of the president (with a heart as big as his assets) I was let in - unofficially - and given the check. I raced home, waved it jubilantly at the men dozing in their truck, and yelled, "I'm certified!" Operation Unload was underway.

Which led to crisis number two.

What was I to do with the load of stuff that wouldn't fit? My place was looking like a furniture mart, and the gigantic moving van was still producing merchandise.

"I guess it's hard to squeeze a four-bedroom house into 1,200 square feet," I said, sprawling on the grass dejectedly.

The movers, pondering the problem while guzzling my beer, came up with, "Get rid of the junk. You could hold a hell of a sidewalk sale, lady."

Pam, twenty-three, unmarried and childless, shrieked, "No! I want my children to have it someday!"

She dashed inside and unearthed the Yellow Pages from beneath a mountain of books in a box. With one phone call, she "let her fingers do the walking."

Then, in many trips, she hauled her future children's inheritance to the Do It Urself Storage Co. In her Honda hatchback. Erself.

Pam always had incredible energy. As a baby she jumped up and down in her crib for hours. My brother, Gershom, said we should have named her, "Pow."

He was right. Even at a young age, whenever I wanted stubborn jars opened or hefty packages carried in, I'd yell, "Pam, I need you," and she'd come running.

She was the perfect one to help me move: the miracle worker who could maneuver furniture, the drill sergeant who'd order order to closets and drawers.

We labored right along with the movers until finally, at the end of the day, even she conked out.

We collapsed together on the sectional (well-grouped in front of the fireplace). Too exhausted to jump up and whoop like she did on the beach, I simply whispered softly, "We did make it, didn't we?"

"Yup," she said, and stretched out flat.

I looked around the room. Surrounded by Illinois furniture, art and china, I felt a trace of sadness mixed with greater parts of joy and relief. The collection from my former life brought back memories of Buddy, but they also represented a sense of substance and stability I'd missed.

I leaned back and stretched my feet out on the round marble table that had belonged to my parents. Suddenly uneasy, I sat up. Was it right to place so much emphasis on things?

I remembered a discussion with Illinois friends about the importance of possessions, and how we all could give them up if we had to. Then, one of us (was it I?) bragged she could pitch a tent anywhere, and be happy. But had I been honest?

I woke Pam to tell her it was bedtime, and asked her, "Could you be happy in a tent?"

"Not tonight I couldn't. Why?"

I told her how once I thought I could.

"But now I'm so happy with all my things, I guess I'm an ugly materialist, after all."

"Mom, don't be so hard on yourself. I dragged everything of mine from home, rescued all that junk to hoard for my kids someday - and I'm glad we're not living in a tent. I love you. Goodnight." Feeling exhonerated I said, "Thanks, honey. I love you too."

On my way to bed, I wound and set the old den clock Buddy and I had bought in Switzerland. With reverence, I placed it on the mantle, and even teared up a bit as I stood back to behold it: familiar friend, serene and already comfortable in its new home.

At the stroke of twelve (twelve strokes to be exact), serenity was shattered.

Pam stalked into my room sputtering, "Mom, that clock was a pain in Illinois, but in this pad, it's Big Ben!"

Sadly, I watched her seize it from the mantle, carry it to the bathroom and wrap thick towels (and a bathmat) around it.

At one o'clock, we heard its lone stifled gong, then fell asleep.

We loved our place.

Over coffee the next morning, I told Pam how challenging it had been to find. Searching for our "special spot," nothing seemed right.

"I tried the guided imagery I'd learned from Hedges and SHAZAM, it appeared . . . a month later."

She smiled.

"It was still a miracle! I knew this condo was right for us the minute I saw the floor plan: one bedroom in the front, one at the rear and lots of space in-between."

"I thought, how perfect (and appropriate) for the two Ms. Melniks who'd be residing there."

"Mom, you were so right." She liked "the plan," too.

Several weeks after Pam and I settled in, fallout began. It's true, Pam was marvelous at moving heavy furniture, but light housekeeping was a different matter.

In my best pleasant voice I tried, "Sweetie, it's your turn to clean this week. I hate to bother you, but when I walk barefoot through the living room, the scuzzballs from the new carpeting get caught between my toes. And I can write my name in the dust on the coffee table."

She peered at me through her sunglasses and replied, "Mom, vacuuming sucks! How can you ask me to clean house on such a gorgeous day? That ocean is one big tidal wave and I feel the pull. Have you seen my bathing suit?"

"It's dangling from the shower head in your bathroom. You could see better if you took your sunglasses off in the house."

"Mom, when you're cool, the sun shines all the time. Why don't you wear shoes in the living room and I'll try to vacuum when I get home."

At the door, she flashed a grin and tossed back, "See ya later."

It became even more difficult to pin Pam down for cleaning chores after she decided to get her master's degree in social work at San Diego State University.

Her standard replies to my not-always-sweet pleas were: "I have to study; it's Saturday; it's Sunday; it's my vacation."

Given those parameters, there could never be a time slot.

Exasperated, I sneezed a lot. I'm allergic to dust – and aggravation.

Pam and Walt met at school in the same program, and they soon began "studying" together. He was over almost every weekend, and we became a "Three's Company" of sorts.

One weekend I announced, "It's time for spring housecleaning."

Pam moaned, "Mom, it's only February." She really hated housework.

Ignoring her, I continued, "I've figured out lists of jobs for everybody to do and I'm posting them on the refrigerator."

Walt said, "Gee it sounds like fun." He must have read *Tom Sawyer* in his youth.

We really dug in. The place was a shambles with the furniture reassembled all over. Pam moved it so Walt could vacuum. I was polishing silver when the phone rang.

It was a friend who asked, "How'd you like to go sailing today?"

I looked over at Pam and Walt and said, "Uh, I don't think

I can make it. I've organized a clean-team here and I'm George Meany. I'd better stick around."

"God, you're doing housework on a day like this? There's a lovely Santa Ana. Warm winds from the desert are calling – can't you hear them?" I laughed and said, "Give me half an hour."

I had to climb over furniture to get to the front door. From beneath my cool sunglasses, I flashed a grin and, mimicking Pam to perfection, tossed back, "See ya later."

Pam lived with me "temporarily" for two years. We still chuckle (and groan) when we look back on that time together.

CHAPTER XVI

A DOCENT TOUR
OF MY ART WORLD

After Pam moved out, I moved on.

A docent at the La Jolla Museum of Contemporary Art, I booked more tours. Joining its Oral History committee kept me busy, too. I interviewed seven people.

Beginning with Donald Brewer, its first director, I learned much about the museum in its early days. I laughed when he told

me that, in addition to his regular duties, he was expected to mow the lawn.

I felt privy to listen in on a part of "olde" La Jolla, when he spun stories about Ellen Browning Scripps he'd heard from people who'd known her.

One of them was how once she asked her maid to lie down on the trolley tracks to keep the trolley from leaving without her. (The route ran right past her house.) He smiled as he added, "the story probably isn't true, but she *was* an extraordinary woman."

Her spacious home abutted the ocean and later became the centerpiece of the museum. To bring it up to "museum quality" after her death, there were many steps From House to Museum, 1897-1996. That's the title of the acknowledgment section in a book, *Learning From LaJolla.* It's the first segment and, written by Hugh M. Davies and Anne Farrell, it's chock full of information about the house and its evolution to a museum. (Ninety-nine years are a lot to cover.)

I studied the book, reviewed my docent training manual and even spoke with Robert Mosher, a well-regarded La Jolla architect. He began the transformation and continued with several others, making most commendable changes. He did, indeed, bring the house up to museum quality.

Bleary-eyed after reading my notes, I decided it's more information than you need to know. Some of the following data is condensed from the before-mentioned sources.

The house was designed by Irving Gill, a pioneer of modern architecture. The last renovation of the museum was completed in 1996. It was done by the highly acclaimed architect-team, Robert Venturi and his wife, Denise Scott Brown. They planned many innovative changes.

One was the creation of a slightly curved stucco wall facade, which reflects the slight curve of the street. That made the museum look more at home in the neighborhood.

Keeping within the limits of the thirty-foot height restriction in La Jolla, they designed an extremely tall ceiling in the lobby with huge star-shaped fins that stretch skyward (but not too far).

There are windows around the top made of clerestory glass with neon inside the space. Natural light streams in during the day. At night, the neon lighting becomes a lantern that beams the museum's presence and beckons people to visit.

*****

I visit often. Volunteering here grew to be a significant part of my life. This museum has become my home-away-from-home. Many people I've met, from Hugh Davies, the director, to

the docents, seem like family. I love "my" museum.

I'm proud to tell you (as I tell all my tour groups), it's the only museum on the planet whose front yard is a neighborhood and whose backyard is an ocean.

I've focused on the history, but it wouldn't be a museum without art. I'm going to tell you about just one piece. (Do I hear a sigh of bas relief?)

It's by Ellsworth Kelly, and the work is titled, "Red Green Blue." It's large, with a big red rectangle on the left and a bigger area of blue (shaped like a huge thumb pointing down) on the right. The background is green. Or seems to be. If you blink... the red and blue shift back, and the green becomes the foreground.

The art is "trompe l'oeil," French for illusion, deception... a trick of the eye.

Life can be trompe l'oeil, too. Often there's an aspect that seems to be dominant, like divorce, and you're foiled into believing it's overwhelming.

By blinking, it's possible to change the picture.

Using guile, I hope to divert your attention from art to me, so I can show you how it changed my world.

I felt honored to be chosen to interview Robert Irwin, an internationally known artist from San Diego. The three hour session was at his home, with frequent interruptions by calls from Malibu. He was the creator of the Central Garden for the new Getty Center, a huge project.

The interview, however, was about the first comprehensive retrospective of his career, held at MOCA (the Museum of Contemporary Art) in Los Angeles.

I'd done my homework, and we delved deeply into his many genres featured in the exhibition. A great artist, he's noted for them all, but especially for his work in light and space. This museum has a stunning glass installation in its permanent collection, among other pieces of his.

But with all his brilliance in so many areas (*The Los Angeles Times* described him as "a man of enormous complexity, drive and energy") . . . what amazed me most was that he was an expert in gardening, too.

****

After interviewing Danah Fayman, a lovely woman prominent in the art world, she asked me to join her board of the San Diego

106

Foundation for the Performing Arts. In addition to learning about dance, I made good friends there, including her.

Through my association with the museum, I met several local artists, among them, Robin Bright and Italo Scanga.

As I began to acquire some of their work, someone asked, "Do you collect?" Trying to be glib, I answered, "No, I pick up." I managed to "pick up" good art I'm proud to own. I even took a sculpting class from Anthony Amato. When I asked him to "appraise" my work, he said, "Good. A-minus." Nobody's perfect.

I joined the University Art Gallery at U.C.S.D. and enjoyed many trips with their travel group.

A writing course I took emphasized "show, don't tell." I found such an array of fun photos. I decided to show them to you, so

you can tell how a blink changed my perspective of life.

"Blink" is a capricious metaphor for that time change. Of course, the transformation took longer than that. But, gratefully, the renovation was less than 99 years!

Actually, the change from my blue period to a rosier one lasted several years. It depends on one's POV (artspeak for point of view.)

Art buffs, by now, I'm sure you realize our journey has been more than a somber stroll through a museum. I "mixed media" with a contemporary collage of my life, and you weren't fooled.

You felt my delight as I sketched the newly-restored me.

You sensed my exhilaration (and even joined in) as our group looked out over the Pacific. We experienced an added dimension of it through Robert Irwin's glass windows. (He'd cut three large holes into them so we could feel the ocean air with our view.)

You caught my enthusiasm as I concluded:
"By stretching my canvas to include new scenery, interests and friends, I not only found a new world ... I discovered a planet!

"You've been a most perceptive group. Thanks for visiting.

"This is the end of the tour."

CHAPTER XVII

FOUR WEDDINGS AND GREAT EXPECTATIONS

I was thrilled when I learned I was to become the "Mother of the Bride" again. And again.

Marcy and Rick had married in 1972, but the other girls were younger and still single.

Now Pam and Walt decided to make their "studying" together legal. They chose July 21st, 1985 for their wedding date.

Soon after their announcement, Peg and Tim called with good news, too. They'd met in Illinois getting their degrees in journalism. After they both became writers, they thought it logical to collaborate. On June 7th, 1986.

Pam and Peg were born fourteen months apart. Now they were each getting married within eleven months. Was it something in the genes?

With the big events approaching, I knew I needed to brush up on weddings. Plural.

I went to Warwick's, the best book store in La Jolla. I wanted a big selection in case I needed several tomes.

I found *Miss Manners' Guide to Excruciatingly Correct Behavior*, with a seventy page chapter on weddings. Amused at the outlandish title, I wanted to know more about the book.

I learned "Miss Manners" was a pseudonym for Judith Martin.

On the cover, just beneath the title, (too excruciating to repeat) was:

"Dear Miss Manners ....

"This is ... a thank-you note for writing such a marvelous book.... your wit and common sense put dear old Amy and Emily to shame....

" Your book deserves to be read by everyone..."

– *The New York Times*

It was a glowing review, but (I'd heard somewhere) you can't tell a book by its cover, so I turned it over.

On the inside page there were two letters:

DEAR MISS MANNERS:
Who says there is a "right" way of doing things and a "wrong"?
GENTLE READER:
Miss Manners does. You want to make something of it?

I liked her attitude.

I flipped to the wedding chapter and loved the essence of her writing: "a wedding should be a jolly gathering of family and friends."

Her common sense approach was perfect for me.

I knew then, her book was the only one I'd need.

*****

Pam and Walt's wedding was held at the Woman's Club in

La Jolla. Just across from the museum, they could see the ocean from the altar in the garden.

We booked it in January, positive there would be no rain in July. (In Illinois that would have been iffy.)

The inside of the club was barn-like. With a furrowed brow, Greta Ross, our wedding planner, suggested that we save money on flowers and rent trees. We chose baskets of in-season daisies for the tables and *lots* of potted ficus trees to "plant" around the room. Greta was a genius.

I thought I'd be nervous to see Buddy and Barbara, but I was fine. Until I was told I'd be following them down the aisle. Uneasy, I hated the idea, and cringed.

Then it was explained, your role in the procession marks your importance in the ceremony.

When I learned I was just before Pam, I felt better.

Lindsay, Marcy and Rick's four-year-old daughter, was the flower girl. She panicked at the last minute and in tears, didn't

want to walk by herself. Unperturbed, Pam gently took her hand and, together, the bride and the flower girl walked down the aisle.

Erin, Lindsay's one-year-old sister, slept soundly on Rick's lap throughout the whole ceremony.

Oh, Pam and Walt's words spoken to each other at the altar were dear and loving.

It was a wonderful wedding.

*****

A few weeks before Peg and Tim's wedding in Illinois, my phone rang.

It was "Great Expectations." The voice was not husky like Beth's, but still Lauren Bacall-ish.

"I see your membership is coming up for renewal. There's a sale on now and we thought you'd like to take advantage of it."

"Wait, I thought my contract was either $300 for one year or $350 for life. I'm sure I paid full price."

"You did, but you didn't read the fine print. After three years, you can still look for someone, but your videotape won't be available for others to see." She added brightly, "If you re-up, you're entitled to make a new video."

I was tired of looking, and had stopped long ago. My feeling had become – if anyone's out there, I want him to find *me*.

Two hundred fifty dollars didn't sound bad. She told me the price was going up to four hundred. Still, with so many wedding bills looming, I decided against it.

As I began packing for my trip to Illinois, I reconsidered. I reasoned that if I did "re-up," it would be like putting my name in a time capsule. It would be there for eternity (even if I weren't). Becoming dramatic, as is my wont to do, I thought a mere two hundred fifty dollars would be a pittance to pay for that. I hoped someone would find me sooner rather than later, but I tried not to expect too much.

Thinking back on my old video, I remembered how sad I was throughout it. I'd even ended by saying, "I loved my husband, and hope to find someone as wonderful as he."

That would be enough to make any viewer's spirit (and more) go limp.

I called "Great Expectations", and asked if the sale was still on.

She replied, "This is the last day."

"Good. Can you put it on my credit card? I want to make a new videotape, but I'll have to schedule it later."

"Fine. Anytime. Thanks for renewing."

*****

It rained on Peg and Tim's wedding day.

We moved the many pots of geraniums from the lovely, now rain-soaked, Millikin Homestead lawn to Southside Country Club. It was our back-up place in case of rain.

The club was not the atmosphere Peg and Tim wanted, but it was dry! And the geraniums placed along the aisle made it seem folksier.

They'd chosen a minister, who turned out to be a disaster.

She had promised to be there early to rehearse, but arrived two hours late! Many of the guests were already seated. Her excuse? She'd been at a hospital visiting a dying man.

Rick said grumpily, "She still could have called."

Peg, already a jittery bride because of the rain and last-minute changes, was so upset that she didn't want to be married by her.

As it happened, Marcus Goodkind, a family friend who'd  performed the service at Pam and Walt's wedding, was now a guest at Peg and Tim's. We knew he was certified to perform marriage in California, but even *he* wasn't sure about Illinois.

At that point, nobody cared!

When Tim was hesitant to fire the minister, Rick, our placid psychologist fumed, "I would love to." And he did.

Marcus performed the ceremony and, legally or not, Peg and Tim were married.

The bar bill was hefty, but as we celebrated together, everyone (even Peg and Tim) moved past the sticky stuff and recognized, "Hey, it was a great wedding."

Marcus had given a profound service, and the guests were all family and close friends genuinely delighted to be there.

"The wedding was the way it was," Werner Erhard would say.

I would say, "Thank God the minister was late."

*****

I had lunch with Buddy the day after the wedding. He was cordial, even loving. We held hands across the table. Our courtship and marriage totaled thirty-six years. It's difficult to discount a relationship that long.

After reminiscing about the past, we moved on to our children, now grown women.

He said, "Francy, we must have done something right. We raised good people."

On that note, we hugged and said goodbye.

Returning home from Illinois, I got back into my routine: tours, meetings and dates (with women or couples).

I saw Pam and Walt often. We lived only thirty minutes apart, depending on traffic, of course.

I felt lucky to have three of my four daughters in California. We continued to coax Peg and Tim to move out, but they both had writing jobs in the Midwest.

Happy with my life, I felt no urgency to call "Great Expectations", especially since the time capsule felt so remote.

But, on a rare, do-nothing day, I called to schedule an appointment for my new videotaping.

*****

This time I was upbeat as I talked about my children, my life and me.

"I'm a writer," I announced proudly. I felt qualified to say it, because I'd had several articles published in the *La Jolla Report*. Granted, it wasn't *The New York Times*, but I was published, by God!

I smiled into the camera and ended with, "I'd like to find someone who will make a meaningful relationship, not a cliché."

When the cameraman gave me two-thumbs up, I knew I had done well.

Before I left, I reviewed my member profile.

The answer to "Who I Am" that I'd written years before:

I'm a composite, like a face on a post office wall drawn from a mix: lively, reflective; serious, hilarious; energetic, exhausted; gregarious, private ... a social person who enjoys a one-on-one with someone I care about and who's even comfortable spending time alone.

"What I'm Looking For"

Long haul: Someone to share concerts, theater, sports, travel, movies and popcorn. Somebody who loves fun and games laced with serious conversation. A guy who prefers a barefoot walk on the beach, but who could fit into a tux for a special occasion.

Short range: Someone to share movies and popcorn.

It may have been a bit dated, but it remained essentially the same.

I left it all for the "time capsule," and went home sighing, "I'm there for posterity."

*****

I got a card in the mail from "Great Expectations." A man named Bill would like to meet me. I gasped, "It's a miracle. Someone's opened the time capsule while I'm still alive!"

I was invited to their quarters to view his videotape and Member Profile. Still in disbelief, I went the next day to make sure it was true.

I watched Bill's video first. He was handsome with white hair, but sadly, a lot older than I. Still, he'd be a nice gentleman to have dinner with occasionally. He had a fun sense of humor I liked.

When I read his Member Profile, I was amazed at the similarities between his and mine.

In the "What I Like To Do" category, he wrote: "I enjoy reading, writing, playing bridge and traveling. I like to be with interesting people, especially those with a sense of humor and who enjoy interesting conversation. I like visiting museums. I enjoy sports and have a twenty-year career in professional baseball, as a player and an executive."

"I'm convinced golf is a game for masochists. If my handicap doesn't improve, I'll probably switch to something easier, like hang-gliding or parachute jumping."

Under "Who I Am," he wrote: "I'm a private person who, with friends, can be warm, friendly and open. Physiologically, I feel at least fifteen years younger than my chronological age. I interact comfortably with people regardless of their age (or mine)."

His answer to "What I'm Looking For" was: "I'd like to meet an attractive, intelligent woman and eventually develop a mutually satisfying one-to-one relationship with her. I'm a one-woman-man. For me, the ideal relationship would be based on mutual respect, genuine friendship, consideration, intimacy and caring."

His Member Profile impressed me more than his videotape. I liked that he felt fifteen years younger than his chronological age. The cleverness and humor in his writing made him seem younger, too.

I knew I'd like to meet him, at least once. From what I saw and read, he seemed charming, and a dinner date with a man now and then would be nice in my life. Before I left, I signed the permission slip they needed to let him know he could call me.

When he phoned, we talked about "Great Expectations," our videotapes and Member Profiles. We agreed we had much in common.

"I read one of the things you like to do is write. Are you writing now?" I asked, trying to move on.

"Yes, I'm working on a manuscript. I'd like to say 'book' but it's not a book until it's published, right?"

"I know. I'm writing a manuscript, too."

"Good. We'll have a lot to talk about on our first date, won't we?"

I felt a flurry of excitement as we planned it. He really sounded nice.

118

Before we hung up, I asked, "Why don't you bring your manuscript along? I'd like to take a look at it."

He said, "Great. I'd like to see yours, too."

I couldn't resist, "So it will be a 'you show me yours and I'll show you mine' sort of thing?"

He laughed and said, "Sounds good!"

When I greeted him at the door, I was surprised at how tall he was. Then I remembered his profile description said, 6'1½".

He'd listed his eyes as green, but I thought they looked more blue. They were twinkling, so it was hard to tell.

He was handsome and he *was* older, but who wouldn't go out with Cary Grant?

We had a lovely dinner at a fine restaurant. Then we went back to my place and talked ... and talked ... and talked. We were just getting to know each other, and there was so much to say.

He told me how impressed he was with my video. He especially liked that I was a writer. "That hooked me," he said with a wink.

I told him about my course, Release the Writer Within You. "It set me on my writer's path, and now, more than ever, I'm sure glad I took it," I said, and winked back.

*****

Bill fit the description perfectly of the member profile I'd filled out at Great Expectations, "What I'm Looking For." Beside the fundamentals, like a guy to share popcorn with at a movie, I'd hoped for someone who could fit into a tux for a special occasion. The tux fit, too.

We began to see each other non-stop.

When he asked me to go to Hawaii with him, I said, "I can't."

"Why not?" he asked, surprised.

"I have to go to Sarasota in November. My brother and sister-in-law are the honorees at a big charity fundraiser. I shouldn't be away so much. I'll miss my tours, meetings .... "

"I thought we'd go in October."

"OK," I relented. "I'll reschedule my life."

If we thought we loved each other before, we truly fell in love at the Mauna Kea. It was sooo romantic. I couldn't believe I'd resisted going.

On the flight home, he said, "I'll miss you when you go to Florida."

"Why not come with me? My mother will be there, too."

I'll never, ever forget it.

The first time Bill met my mother, she was sitting on a couch in my brother's home. He sat down beside her, kissed her and said, "Hi, Mom."

We were married on February 1st, 1987, five months after our first date.

*****

Miss Manners would not have approved. I moved in with Bill the December before we were married.

His place was huge. Bill had been a builder and developer, and the last building he built was Del Prado, on Sixth and Upas across from the north end of Balboa Park. He had been smart enough to save the top floor for himself, so ... that made it a penthouse with a 360° view!

When my kids urged me to conclude my manuscript with Bill and our new life together, I said, "That's impossible. Who'd believe it? I don't even believe it myself."

It hadn't fully penetrated when Bill wrote in his Member Profile, "I combined a twenty-year career in baseball as a player and executive," it meant he started out as a catcher with the San Diego Padres and moved on to become the principal owner. It was when the Padres were a minor coast league team, but still impressive. He'd moved from the ground floor *up*.

Living there was fabulous. In disbelief, I'd walk around his place in the middle of the night, or the middle of the day, or any time at all and gaze at the views: downtown San Diego, the bay, the Coronado Bridge ... even Mexico. I was a lucky woman, indeed.

But the grandest part of my new life was Bill. I loved him

tremendously – from the very beginning ... and before I read the fine print of his life.

Planning our wedding together was fun. It was to be at our home, and with only children and grandchildren. That's the way Bill wanted it, and I agreed.

We both had brothers, sisters and their families. Lists can become complicated, as Miss Manners well knows. We felt right choosing intimacy.

I felt sad about not including my mother, but there was a reason for that. February in San Diego can be cold, not harsh like most places, but certainly cooler than Florida, where Mom lived. We talked to her about it and she admitted it made sense. Coming out in the spring would be a better time for us to celebrate belatedly.

A few weeks later, I changed my mind. I told Bill I felt my mother should be at our wedding and he said, "You're absolutely right. Phone her immediately and invite her."

When I called to tell her that both Bill and I wanted her to come to our wedding, she didn't respond.

"Can't you hear me? We want you to be with us to celebrate at the time, not in the spring."

She was still mute. "Mom, what's the matter? Don't you want to come?"

She began laughing hard, and finally sputtered, "I'm coming. I'll be there! It's all arranged."

She had called Rick for his professional opinion about her coming, uninvited.

His response was, "Gommy, you're ninety-two years old. If you want to go to your daughter's wedding, I think it's appropriate for you to be there."

She had consulted with my brother and sister, too. Both were in total agreement with Rick's "analysis."

She next called Pam and Walt to see if she could stay with them. She told them she didn't want to intrude upon us in any way.

The whole family knew.

My mother was "crashing" our wedding and wanted to surprise us!

I put Bill on the phone to hear the story from her. He hung up, grinning. "What a woman!" he said. "I'm glad she'll be here." Laughing through tears, I said, "Me, too."

* * * * *

Peg and Tim arrived from the Midwest a few days before the wedding. Bill and I met them at the airport, not far from our "aerie."

Peg was bobbing a huge placard above her head which read, "ALMOST MARRIED," while throwing confetti wildly at Bill and me. People all around us were laughing. Bill looked at me, horrified. I forgot to tell him she was rambunctious.

Oops, I had forgotten to tell *her* how reserved Bill was, especially in public places. I went home thinking, "Poor Peg. How will she wiggle her way out of this?"

After hustling up food for lunch, I popped into the den to tell everyone it was ready and, Oh my God! There was Bill sitting in  his big leather chair with Peg on his lap.

They were chatting amiably, as if they'd known each other for years. (Actually, they'd just met.)

Who knew what voodoo Peg conjured up to absolve her no-no? The fact was, like magic, it worked.

* * * * *

Bill wore an ivory tie, I wore a pink wool dress, and Mother was radiant in her red silk.

Our children and grandchildren were all there, just as we'd wished.

After our families left and we were alone on the deck, Bill raised his glass in a toast to "Great Expectations."

I kissed him and whispered, "Thanks for rescuing me from the time capsule."

*****

Shortly after Bill and I were married, we got a call from Amy and Steve. After dating for several years, they decided to get married, too. During the four-way conversation, we told them how excited we were and, newlyweds ourselves, welcomed them to our world.

Steve was the boy next door – literally. In L.A. the chances of marrying your next-door neighbor are miniscule (certainly far less than in Saint Louis.)

The wedding was to be September 5th, 1987. Their first task was to find a place to have it. Exploring L.A., they didn't like the atmosphere at the big hotels.

When Bill heard that, he suggested to me, "Why don't they take a look at the party room here in the building?"

Amy and Steve came down for the weekend to check it out.

The room was designed for large occasions, had a full kitchen and a deck with a view. They liked it immediately. They were lucky, too. It was available on the Saturday night of Labor Day weekend. The contract signed, we went up to our place to celebrate.

Bill brought out Akvavit from the freezer and the four of us sat at the dining room table, said, "skoal," and sipped it slowly ... for a long time.

Three hours later we cancelled dinner reservations, ate tuna melts at home and conked out early. Our evening had been less than scintillating.

But, as I vaguely recall .... we had a jubilant afternoon toasting to Amy and Steve's party room for their wedding.

"Mother of the Bride" (with hope, for the last time), I pulled out Miss Manners' book yet again. It seemed heavier. Was I weary? The dog-eared book looked exhausted, too.

None-the-less, Judith, Amy and I managed to strike a good balance between proper protocol and California casual for the occasion. (Judith was "Miss Manners," but by then we were on a first name basis.)

*****

Amy and Steve looked like the bride and groom on top of a wedding cake. They were a handsome couple.

It was a festive affair with family and guests from Illinois and L.A. People stayed for a long time. The band was great.

Bill grew weary, excused himself, and went up to bed.

Buddy was there without Barbara and asked me to dance. Our daughters all wept, we found out later. (We danced closely.)

I hosted four "jolly gatherings" in two years, and one of them was mine!

Now all the girls were married. All five of us.

Steve's son, Jason, was his junior best man.

CHAPTER XVIII

THE WRITE STUFF

After Amy and Steve's wedding, Bill and I returned to our project. Bill was finishing his manuscript, now with my help.

I had status because I had taken writing courses, attended writers conferences and had written for the "La Jolla Report." I even did a cover story, "First Person Singular: The Single Scene … Sad and Sweet."

When Pat Dahlberg read it, she told me, "Francy, I think you have a book in you." I took it as a compliment, but brushed it off with, "The singles subject is therapeutic for me to write about."

At writers conferences in Santa Barbara, I learned much. The atmosphere was like camp, folksy and fun. Some of the "folks" were Ray Bradbury, pictured top-middle on the next page, the science fiction writer (famous for *The Illustrated Man, Fahrenheit 451* and *The Martian Chronicles)* and Charles Schulz, whom everyone called "Sparky." Jonathan Winters obliged with a smile when I asked him for his autograph.

Sparky and his wife, Jean, stayed in the cabin next to mine and often we'd leave at the same time to go up to breakfast. I'd say, "Hi neighbors," and we'd walk together. Later, when he died, I felt the same huge loss as the rest of the world, but especially sad to lose my "neighbor." (Schulz was the creator of the comic stip, "Peanuts.")

Charles Champlin, Critic-at-Large for *The Los Angeles Times,*

was there, too. He loved the nudist colony chapter of my manuscript, and asked me to read it to his workshop two consecutive years. I was flattered.

In his column for *The Times*, July 1st, 1986, "Learning About the Write Stuff," he wrote about that summer's conference which included a paragraph about me:

"One of the week's more interesting readings was from a manuscript by a newly divorced, middle-aged woman seeking a new life in Southern California and exploring all the nostrums from est to nudism available beside the Pacific. The writer put an amusing face on a fairly universal and painful process of readjustment." I was touched.

My credentials for helping Bill with his manuscript soared

when I called Charles Champlin. After hearing Bill's subject was baseball, he said, "let me talk to him." (Chuck was an avid fan of the game.) They gabbed about the sport and, with instant comradery, he asked Bill to send him his manuscript.

That began a barrage of letters and calls between them. Chuck was eager to help, and did.

*****

Bill's book was published in 1989. The cover read:

Clearing the Bases
Baseball Then & Now
By Bill Starr

A professional account of old time and new time baseball revealing:
Baseball in the roaring twenties and thirties.

And many fascinating insights into how baseball was played, and is played today.

Forward by
Ralph Kiner

The book started with acknowledgements to those who gave him professional guidance and encouragement.

Typical of Bill, he began with the librarian at the Mission Hills branch of the San Diego libraries. Then, among others he thanked were Jimmy Reese, Ralph Kiner and Charles Champlin.

The last paragraph read:

"And a big hug to my wife, Francy, a former high school English teacher who can grasp a sentence in midflight, rearrange the tenses, remove the qualifiers, reorganize the clauses and hand it back as a finished product before I can say, 'Hold the English lesson!'"

His inscription to me in the book softened the mock rebuke:
" To Francy – my wife – my friend,
Without your confidence, persuasion, guidance and tireless effort, this book would never have been completed and published.
With appreciation and all my love, Bill."

Delighted with the tribute, I felt especially honored to be his wife – and friend.

Ralph Kiner's forward began with a newspaper item he recalled about Bill in early 1956. It was written by Jack Murphy, the nationally prominent sports editor of "The San Diego Union."

Jack was interviewing Leslie O'Conner, who'd been assistant to commissioner, "Happy" Chandler, and who later became the lawyer for the Pacific Coast League.

Jack wrote, "The interview turned to the subject of Bill Starr. O'Conner was especially outspoken in his admiration of Bill." Then he quoted O'Conner, "To my notion, Bill Starr was the keenest mind in baseball. Nobody was a better judge of playing talent, and he was unsurpassed as a negotiator. When I say he was the smartest man in baseball, I don't exclude anybody. I rate him over George Weiss of the Yankees, over Frank Lane, of the Cardinals, over all of 'em."

Bill was astounded and proud of O'Conner's assessment. I was too. (I knew Bill was great, I didn't know he was the greatest!)

There were laudatory blurbs on the back cover by Tommy Lasorda, manager of the Los Angeles Dodgers; Roger Kahn, author of *The Boys Of Summer;* and Charles Champlin. The last,

Ralph Kiner, telecaster for the New York Mets, wrote (from the forward):

"...The most informative, penetrating book on baseball I have ever read...chronicled by an expert who tells it like it is, and was."

*****

There was a book-signing evening at Warwick's with many people attending, including Bill's granddaughter Jenna (pictured on page 129). Even his longtime baseball chum, Buzzie Bavasi was there. A party hosted by friends followed. Bill was truly a star. We celebrated his celebrity with a trip.

We returned to find letters of congratulations about his book. He was ecstatic when he got one from his good pal, Ted Williams. (Bill was proud to claim he was the only player who pinch-hit for him. It was a fluke, but that's another story.)

Even with all the praise and best wishes, his book received only a modicum of commercial success. I guess he was too many generations back to interest the current baseball fans.

At least he lived to celebrate his achievement: a published book.

CHAPTER XIX

BOXES

Buddy died first, in August 1990. He was sixty-three.

Our daughters were all planning to return to Illinois for the funeral.

Even though I was married to Bill, I decided to go with them. I'm not sure Bill understood why, until I explained, "he's the father of my four children and I want to be with our girls at their father's funeral."

They were each getting a family bereavement rate, and when I called the airline to purchase my ticket, I asked for one, too.

"Are you his wife?" asked the ticket agent.

"No. But I was for thirty-one years and we dated for five years before that...and he's the father of my four children, and..."

She interrupted me, saying, "I have no authority to issue that rate to you. Would you like to speak to my supervisor?"

"Yes. Please."

When the supervisor finally got on the line, I began repeating my story, but she stopped me.

"The agent already explained and we both agree. You qualify."

He was buried on August 29th, the same date we were married.

*****

Bill died the next year, in August, too.

We had moved to La Jolla in April not knowing until moving day that he was ill.

His obituary was appropriately in the sports section.

But Bill's picture was over the masthead of "The San Diego Union" with these words,

"Star of Early Padres Dies," in bold type.

Under that, "Bill Starr, 80, won pennants as both a player and an owner."

When Buddy died, I couldn't cry. I'd shed all my tears during the divorce period. My real sadness was for my daughters who'd lost their father.

With Bill's death, I mourned deeply. Even after acknowledging intellectually that death is a part of life, I found "stoic" was not my forte. Following Dan Kiley's advice helped: "Don't wallow in your grief. Allow it for a time, then move on." (I often splurged on the minutes.)

Remembering the wisdom of my dear friend, Hedges Capers (who'd passed away, too) was more comforting.

Years earlier, when I asked him about dealing with loss, he responded, "You must have wonderful memories."

After I nodded, yes, he said softly, "Then you'll always have them, won't you?"

Shortly after Bill died, a woman who had just met me asked, "Are you a divorcée or a widow?"

I said, "Yes."

*****

Condolence cards, letters, and notices of charity donations in Bill's honor started to accumulate. Also data about Bill's book, his press clippings and my paragraph from the "L.A. Times" began to clutter.

I've always been a pack rat. I still had a large manila envelope labeled, "Things I'm Afraid to Throw Away."

It was time to organize. Marcy came down to jump start the project. We found 9"x15" boxes, cardboard, but sturdy, with racks like file drawers. They were perfect.

Still in mourning, I gathered everything about Bill and piled it all into three deep drawers. It was too difficult for me to begin there.

Thinking "first things first," in my structured mind-set, I decided to start with my four daughters and their families. They had accumulated, too.

Marcy and Rick came first, with files for each of them.

Lindsay and Erin had separate files, too. "General Family" was at the back.

The same procedure was used for all their boxes. Amy was followed by Steve, Tanner and Alex.

Pam came next, with Walt, Kate and Drew.

Peg was the fourth box. (Remember? She was my fourth child, fourth daughter, born on April fourth.) Her file was followed by Tim and Sophie Tucker. Let me explain.

Their children were born eight years apart. When Peg announced they were going to name their new son, "Tucker," I told her, "There was a red hot Mama named 'Sophie Tucker.' How can you do that?"

"Mom, no one will ever say their names together like hers."

I do.

When I call Peg and Tim, I ask, "What's new with Sophie Tucker?"

"My bad," as my grandchildren would say.

As you can see from their picture, the acorns don't fall far from the apple tree.

Bill used to love it when I mixed my metaphors.

I missed his laugh.

*****

The "Immediate Family Box" began with my parents, and along with our family tree, rooting wildly, I included Buddy's. Jack and Pearl, were my second mother and father and we were all close.

When Bill and I married, we received a check from Mom Melnik. The card was to me, "You'll always be my daughter." Bill couldn't believe we'd received a wedding gift from Buddy's mother.

My brother, Gershom, wrote many loving letters to family throughout the years. To commemorate his ninety-fifth birthday, his daughter, Vicki, and her husband, Howard, compiled them. With Arlene and David, his other children, and David's wife, Jean, they published *A Wise and Loving Heart.* It was a total surprise to him, and he wept when he saw the book.

His emotions run the gamut from sentimentality to droll humor. An item written about him in a Sarasota newspaper included his photo and these words: "Debonair philanthropist and man-about-town, Gersh Cohn, threw himself a 100th birthday party. Cohn, a mere 95, said he wants to enjoy it and he's not sure he'll make it."

He has macular degeneration, but still plays duplicate bridge three times a week. We talk every day.

My sister, Estelle, who was a Marine in World War II, just turned ninety, and is amazing. She works out regularly at the

La Jolla Y doing strenuous exercises with her trainer. She loves to show off her Popeye muscles. She's had much adversity in her life and, besides loving her, I admire her inner strength.

She's been involved in the art world, too – in Chicago on the boards of Steppenwolf Theater and Hubbard Street Dance Company, to name a few, and here at the La Jolla Playhouse.

Gersh and Estelle, with their families, are "boxed" separately.

It seems we three "children" inherited longevity from Mother. Every five years, the family celebrated her birthdays with especially big parties. What fun! There were many. Here we are at her 90th.

When she reached 100, we celebrated with seven parties. One was a wine and cheese at my home.

On the dining room table I put a portrait of her taken when she was a young woman, a cake with a replica of it on the icing, and a bowl of green bananas. She used to kid, "At my age, I don't buy green bananas." I thought it fun to include them. (She did too.)

Mom stood in front of my fireplace and, grinning, told us all how grateful she was to be there for the occasion. After the laughter stopped, she spoke a bit about her lucky life, then thanked everyone for coming.

I was so proud of her. She lived her life with spirit, vitality, and determination. (Learning to drive at seventy-two is no easy task.)

Here's another 100th birthday picture with Gershom's lovely wife, Sylvia, who passed away in 2006.

Debby and her sister, Jan, are together in the "Extended Family" box. I often introduce Debby with this one-liner, "we're sisters-in-law twice removed - we're both divorced from brothers."

I love her like a sister.

Jan's last name is Shakowsky. She's a Congresswoman from Illinois and a long-time friend of Obama. (I've known her since she was eight.)

I first met Obama in 2006 at the La Jolla home of a friend, Christine Forester. The occasion was a fundraiser for the Democratic Party. Unsure what to say to him as he approached me, I came up with, "I'm from Illinois, too, and we have a mutual friend."

Curious, he asked, "Who?"

When I said, "Jan Shakowsky," he hugged me enthusiastically and said, "If it weren't for Jan, I wouldn't have been elected." He meant for state senator of Illinois.

We met a second time at another fundraiser. I got there hours early to get a front row position. As he approached the lectern, I shouted, "Jan Shakowsky!"

He looked down at me and laughed, "You again?" I got my second hug.

Three daughters, two granddaughters, Jan, Debby and I were present at his inauguration. Although the weather was below freezing, we bundled together and felt warmer sharing those moments in history with our own "delegation."

(Pictured below, Jan is to my right and Debby is crouched in front. Lindsay missed the pic.)

Debby and I attended the Illinois Ball, too. When President Obama appeared on the stage, I stifled a huge urge to shout out Jan's name. I knew it would have been inappropriate. (But I did want him to know I was there.)

The man in the picture with Obama and me is Marvin. We knew each other from the art world, but only began going out together six and a half years after Bill died.

It took me another six months to "get serious" in the relationship.

139

I truly just wanted to go out to dinner occasionally with this nice gentleman. He, like Bill, was much older than I.

But one night we dined at the Marine Room which, as you might suspect, overlooks the ocean. A rare phenomenon, called the green flash, occurred at sunset. We drank champagne to celebrate.

Later that night, I succumbed to his charm, telling him, "Any man who can create the green flash is too powerful for me."

We had the best of two worlds. Sometimes I was with him at his place. More often, he was with me at mine. Then we realized we had the best of three worlds. Sometimes he'd be at his condo and I'd be home alone. (We traveled well together, though.)

It was a sweet relationship. My family adored him and I loved

his family too. His cute granddaughters, Portia and Adrienne, are pictured below.

We never married, although I referred to him as my three-quarters husband.

We were together nine and a half years, until he died in 2007.

I added Marvin to the "Husbands" box with Buddy and Bill. I figured I loved them all and they all loved me. They'd have a lot in common.

Each of their families has "adopted" me. Beyond feeling grateful, I take comfort in just being with them. We have a lot in common, too.

Some of the other boxes are "Friends," "Trips" and "My Manuscript." It was the first time since I moved to California that I'd catalogued my life.

I grieved for the dear ones I'd loved and lost.

But it was consoling to know they were all on file where I could find them.

CHAPTER XX

BOOK ENDS

I loved my brother's book. The back cover headlines: "Words of Wisdom From Gersh Cohn." If there were wise words from others, like the man he sat next to on a plane ... or Buddha, he'd add his spin and they'd become topics for the epistles I dubbed: "The World According to Gersh."

Reading his book inspired me to rethink *my* words. The manuscript I wrote had lain dormant for almost thirty years. After I married Bill and my girls urged me to finish it, I'd said, "Impossible - who'd believe it?" So happy living my life, I had no desire to write about it.

And always torn between the private sector and the public domain, I'd squirm at the thought of even my family reading it ... my grandchildren? Heaven forbid! What about my indiscretions and the X-rated stuff? How about the reaction of the general public?

Baring my soul seemed comparable to nudism. Would it be easier with people I knew or total strangers?

The Auntie Mame within me sensed my dilemma, but chuckled, "What the hell? Go for it! At our age, who cares?"

I pulled out my manuscript from its hibernation and thumbed through the pages.

Laughing at my capers, I made the decision to finish it. But where should I start? With my quirk for chronology, I thought, where better than at the beginning?

Reading those early chapters of sulking and seeking, I began to reassess ... and recap.

Beginning with my dizzy bicycle spin down the singles path, I covered a lot of territory. My bike lurched in all directions, and so did I.

Separated from my past, I was lonely (especially on a Sunday). In denial, I refused to say the "D" word aloud, yet realized I needed to find a future without Buddy. That was a lot to juggle.

Maybe that's why I lost my balance.

Werner Erhard's explanation of est equates it with bicycle riding, "You know about balancing in a certain way. If you fall off...." The rest of his quote, like Miss Manners' title, is too excruciating to repeat. (It's in the est chapter on page 77 if you want to re-read it.) Bottom line: It was a puzzle.

I decided to put the pieces together. I wanted to fit in everything (as you know).

Piecing my life together wasn't easy, but I had an advantage. Being unknown in San Diego felt like a protective shield that gave me the courage to abandon prudence, and plunge.

Those good at solving jig-saw puzzles understand that the best plan is to start from the outer edge and work inward.

I started at the outré edge, all right!

I began with the most outrageous experience of my life. If I hadn't been encouraged by all that anonymity bravado, I *never* would have played a bit part in a cheeky scene at a nudist colony!

Yet being "far out" jolted me into reality. I began to let go of the past and lighten up. (Caution: Do *not* try this in your hometown.)

Another outlandish experience was the "Firewalk." Without ever having a burning desire to walk barefoot over hot coals, I did it. It was an extreme technique of demonstrating that the utmost is possible. I felt a warm glow knowing that if I could do that, I could do anything. Seriously (despite the punning), I learned I had power.

The out-of-body experience I felt at est made me realize I was responsible for myself.

After being told we had choices, and that inability to choose keeps us stuck, I chose to get unstuck without coming unglued, and take charge of my life.

Another part of the forty percent I got from est: "Obviously the truth is what's so. Not so obvious is, it's also so what?"

That impelled me forward more than anything! I learned there was nothing I could do to change the past. Nothing. So there was nothing to do but move on. That was a huge push.

Rebirthing was a push, too. I felt a tremendous surge of gratitude to be alive. As a "newborn," I began sniffing life in a fresh way.

The nudist colony, I believe, is still there, but I never went back. I barely made it the first time.

I'm not sure if est and "The Firewalk Experience" are in existence, but their concepts are: Conquer fear and use the power to move on.

I won my struggle to survive a devastating divorce. The paths I took to recovery ranged from rugged to hilarious, as you've read. Twice.

Oh, I did complete the puzzle. The innermost pieces I inserted were these general truths:
- Most people associate risk with making a change.
- Sometimes *not* making a change can be a risk.
- Adding gleams to your goals can lighten the way.
              The "centerpiece?"
- Divorce needn't be deadly. Good may even come from it.

*****

The puzzle solved, I moved on with my life and stopped writing about it. In 1983 my exit line was to Pam, "See ya later."

My decision to restore and complete this "evolution from manuscript to book" was in 2011. Recapping the past and writing anew, I relived sad memories, but I survived. Twice.

Getting close to closure (do you say winding up or winding down?) I'd like to close with an update of my family and my life as it is.

Mother moved here from Florida and lived in a retirement community for her last seven years.

At ninety-five, she attended my sixtieth birthday party Bill hosted on our deck. Her "date" was Mandell Weiss, Bill's friend.

I remember her as she's pictured, smiling.

In her later years, she had a "sweetheart." They pulled their wheelchairs close every day and held hands. She smiled then, too.

Somewhere, perhaps in a greeting card, I read that approaching old age, one needs "grit, grace, gratitude and attitude." Mom had them all. (She lived to be 102.)

I like to think those qualities are in my genes. I'm not approaching old age. I'm there. Statistically. But as Bill wrote in his Member Profile, he felt fifteen years younger than his age. So do I.

Mother's move to California moved others to follow.

Estelle and Hammy breezed in from the "windy city" for calm retirement. We welcomed them into our California clan.

Peg and Tim wended their way from the Midwest to Santa Rosa. Even though they're North and the rest of us are South, we're all West ... and in the same state. At last!

Then mass production accounted for six new grandchildren. The eight of them now range from thirty-one to twelve. I'm Granny Franny to them all, even Lindsay, the eldest.

Bill, and later Marvin, were part of my life during many of those years, too.

Now, with the preponderance of my family in California (we increased from one to twenty-one) I'm not lonely anymore. On *any* day.

It's become tradition for us to gather at Pam and Walt's for the Thanksgiving holiday. Their home, because of its location and size, has become our family abode for other occasions, too.

Pam and Walt are happy. They don't have to travel far.

My grandchildren are delighted. The cousins love being together. Most of the pictures of them all are taken there - in order of their ages, of course.

Sparing you more of "all in the family," I'll get you up to speed (pun intended) about just Pam. Remember? She lived with me temporarily ... for two years.

She and Walt have a twenty-three year old daughter, Kate, and a son, Drew, nineteen.

Pam has been ready for her future grandchildren for twenty years with a huge cabinet filled with dolls, toys and games. Some of the "heirlooms" she'd saved for them from the Do It Urself Storage Company are included.

She's President and CEO (what else?) of the large retirement community where Mother lived. Because it's near her home, she doesn't have to travel far.

And she still doesn't vacuum.

*****

"There are no accidents in the universe. You are exactly where you are meant to be," I was told at est.

I didn't believe it then. I do now.

Looking for the best place to live during a trial separation, I'd thought of our dog, Oliver, who wound around in a circle until he found the perfect place to plop.

I circled around, too, and found La Jolla.

The next day, I drove ten miles south to San Diego. After choosing brochures at their Chamber of Commerce, the man behind the desk asked, "Are you going to be here long?"

I felt goose bumps on my arms as I answered, "Maybe the rest of my life." I'm still here, exactly where I'm meant to be, feeling goose bumps again as I'm writing.

Like Oliver, I found my perfect spot.

There is so much available to enjoy in this wonderful combination of village and city. Besides visiting my museum, I attend concerts and theater at The Athenaeum, The La Jolla

Playhouse, The Old Globe, The San Diego Symphony and The La Jolla Music Society.

I pared that list with a machete. There are many other venues I could name, like the The San Diego Opera, The San Diego Youth Symphony (fabulous) and the famous San Diego Zoo my grandchildren love. The list goes on... but I won't. I just wish I

could distribute their brochures to you all. Do I sound like the Chamber of Commerce?

On an extraordinary day, I have lunch with Obama. It was an honor to be hugged recently by the President of the United States ... and fun to catch up with my old "pal," who'd hugged me twice before, when he was a senator.

On an ordinary day, I see friends, play duplicate bridge or write a book.

Of course, my dear family stays close. You can see how my sons-in-law adore me.

I love my life and I'm grateful for it. As I wrote before, I'm a lucky woman, indeed.

"You create your own luck," my brother would say,

I would say, "I skittered across the coals, and made it."

To readers not in the "Immediate Family" box, much of this book must have seemed like viewing a home movie of a trip you didn't take. (Be grateful I didn't inflict upon you the eight millimeter films I took of mountains on my honeymoon.)

Thanks for tolerating the home flicks. If you perceived other views along the way, I'm pleased.

For anyone facing divorce (or other loss) perhaps you gained insights that may help you through it.

To you who just came along for the bicycle ride, I hope you enjoyed the spin. Even though you're not in the family, please know, if you bought my book, you're adopted.

You who *are* family have taken the road more traveled. Although I made my journey alone, you were with me, in spirit, every step of the way. I love you all.

Winding *up* as this book ends, skoal to everyone who made it to the finish line. Thanks for sticking with me when I was stuck.

ADDENDUM

A FAMILY PHOTO ALBUM

Even spared my movies of mountains, it's still likely you're too bleary-eyed to look at more pictures. Yet, I found such an "array of fun photos," I thought perhaps family (and those adopted) might want to take a peek at these pics arranged in random, haphazard, hodge-podge disorder!

Fishkel and Eelbert

"Two Fins Up" Theater

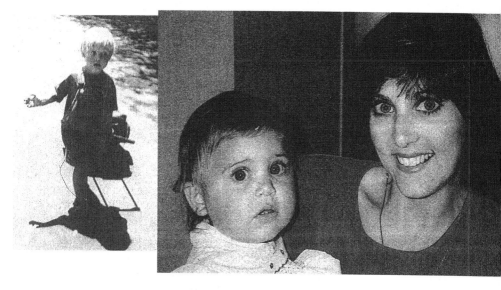

ACKNOWLEDGMENTS

Enormous love and thanks to my four daughters, Marcy, Amy, Pam and Peggy, who when asked for their approval or disapproval of my writing ... gave me both.

To my brother, Gershom, our family's debonair guru, who was wise enough to create bright children who compiled his letters to us into a published book, which inspired me to finish mine.

To my sister, Estelle, and her husband, Hamilton, who called from Chicago (especially on a Sunday) to listen at length to the drivel of the early chapters I was living.

To Charles Champlin who taught me the Write Stuff; how to grasp a flawed sentence in mid-flight and fix it. Thanks, Chuck, for your help with Bill's book, too.

To Hedges Capers who asked me if I had a belly-button and, after my nod, explained, "That makes you human, doesn't it?"

To my graphic designer and publisher at Merlin Design, Howard Evans, for his dedicated work on my "work in progress" to make sure it progressed ... in the right direction.

Thanks to all the others who helped me glue this book together, especially Hugh Davies, Robert Mosher, Joy Wolf, Liz Yamada, Harriette Buckman, David Cohn, Che Sweetland, Catherine Palmer and Mark Walker (a man I sat next to on a plane).

Designed and produced in Blue Hill ME
by
Merlin Design

http://merlin-design.net

Made in the USA
Lexington, KY
30 August 2012